THE ERNST CASSIRER LECTURES

THE ACTOR
AND THE SPECTATOR

Lewis White Beck

NEW HAVEN AND LONDON, YALE UNIVERSITY PRESS, 1975

Designed by Sally Sullivan
and set in Baskerville type.
Printed in the United States of America by
The Colonial Press Inc., Clinton, Massachusetts

Published in Great Britain, Europe, and Africa by
Yale University Press, Ltd., London.
Distributed in Latin America by Kaiman & Polon,
Inc., New York City; in India by UBS Publishers' Distributors Pvt.,
Ltd., Delhi; in Japan by John Weatherhill, Inc., Tokyo.

*Great commotion among the spectators; a few cry,
others laugh; others, embarrassed, sneeze.*

Scaevola. It's not to be put up with, that's for sure. Look, friends, here we sit as spectators and watch a play; spectators sit in that play and watch a play, and then yet another play is performed in this third play before those actors now thrice metamorphized.

Wachtel. Just to put my mind at rest I'd gladly be an actor in that last comedy. The farther from the spectator, the better.

The other man. Consider this, friends: maybe we ourselves are actors in some play, and someone else is watching this completely mixed-up stuff. Then we'd be the first play. Maybe this is the way the angels see us.

Ludwig Tieck, *Die verkehrte Welt* (original version, 1798), end of act III.

CONTENTS

PREFACE

This book is my attempt to explain how human beings understand each other and themselves. I contrast and assess two ways of doing so: the commonsense and the scientific. To this end I arrange simple episodes in which one person is observed by two others and each tells what is going on.

One of the spectators is a little like Dickens's Mr. Gradgrind, "with a rule and a pair of scales, and the multiplication table always in his pocket, sir, ready to weigh and measure any parcel of human nature, and tell you exactly what it comes to." I make him say some things that C. D. Broad remarked would be said only by "a fool or a physiologist." But believing with Aristotle that drama (he says tragedy) is more philosophical than history, I have tried to create a character whose actions are not guided by what he knows as a man and to let him speak as if he were a true-blue scientific observer and nothing else. I know some scientists who try to talk like him, though cheerfulness is always breaking in. My straw man in a lab coat helps me in setting up a contrast that brings out, more clearly than actual life could, the implications of the diverse ways in which men seek understanding.

The book is based upon, and largely identical with, the Cassirer Lectures delivered at Yale University in November 1974. Unlike many in my audience, I never did meet Cassirer. His *Substance and Function* was the first serious philosophical work I ever studied seriously; it was almost my introduction to philosophy. Eight years after reading it, I saw him; but not wishing to play Briggs to his Napier, I did not present myself to him. As my admiration for his work has grown and my diffidence diminished, I have regretted more and more that I did not take that opportunity to meet him, especially since I have been told by those who did know him that he would have welcomed words with a young and unknown philosopher. The influence of Cassirer on my thought is visible in almost all my writings, and I like to think that he would not have disagreed very much with what I say in these lectures dedicated to his memory.

My visit to Yale was memorable to me for the interested attention of my audiences and for the friendly hospitality of colleagues and friends. I am grateful to Mrs. Roslyn Yaravitz for the skill and alacrity with which she prepared my manuscript for the press.

L.W.B.

December 1, 1974
Rochester, New York

1: CAN A HUMAN MACHINE

THINK?

More urgently, perhaps, than ever before in our history, two models compete for employment in efforts to understand man. One is old and no longer excites. It is based on the ideal of man as autonomous and self-creating, expressed in God's apostrophe to Adam in Pico della Mirandola's *Oration on the Dignity of Man*:

> Neither a fixed abode nor a form is thine alone nor any function peculiar to thyself have I given thee to the end that according to thy longing and judgment thou mayest possess whatever abode, form, and functions thou desirest. The nature of all other beings is limited and constrained within the bounds of laws . . . but thou, constrained by no limits . . . shalt ordain for thyself the limits of thy nature. We have set thee in the world's center that thou mayest observe whatever is in the world. As though the moulder and maker of thyself, thou mayest fashion thyself into whatever shape thou shalt prefer. To thee is granted to do whatever thou choosest, to be whatever thou wilt.

The other is the scientific conception of man as a cog in the machinery of the world or as the loose screw in the universe that, with proper techniques, can be tightened up, so that the "play" in the universe is reduced to plan and order and so that men can manage their affairs better when they give up the illusion that they can put all things under their feet by keeping them on a cloud.

The humanistic ideal, an expression of *hybris* in the Greek world and again in the fifteenth century, now seems to social engineers conservative, traditional,

obscurantist, and ineffective in men's dealing with
each other. The proponents of the scientific model of
man in turn appear to the humanist to suffer from
hybris, to be brash, iconoclastic, and technocratic but
frighteningly effective in the engineering of social
change.

I fear there may be some truth in each of these
caricatures. It might have gone better with man, "der
kleine Gott der Welt" Goethe calls him in *Faust,* had
he not been given "den Schein des Himmelslichts; Er
nennts Vernunft und brauchts allein/Nur tierischer als
jedes Tier zu sein"—but even Goethe could not have
dreamt of the brutal degradation that technocratic
men have brought upon themselves and each other in
our century. So much, then, for the fruitfulness of
men's idealistic illusions about themselves and their
fellows. But, in turning to those who would save us
from our old myths about ourselves, we find new
utopias that are unwittingly frightful.

Notice one thing about the prerogative assigned to
man by Pico's God: "We have set thee in the world's
center that thou mayest observe whatever is in the
world." One of the highest creations of man is science,
which lays bare nature's secrets but which depicts
human beings as things, finally as things without
dignity and freedom. The institution of science is
Janus-like. In its internal, self-imposed controls on
intellectual vagaries, waywardness, and arbitrariness
and in its intellectual and moral discipline it is one of
the loftiest manifestations of the spiritual values of
mankind: it is the programmatic aspect of the Miran-
dolan archetype. But in its results, while giving men

power, it demeans them in their own eyes and threatens their future. The Janus-head embodies man as seer and man as seen, man as actor and man as acted upon. This conjunction of two models competing for use while they are themselves interlocked and interdependent—this is the phenomenon I wish to understand.

With few exceptions even in medicine, the methods and conceptions developed in the study of nature were seldom before the seventeenth century applied to the human body, mind, and society; Lucretius was little followed. It was more characteristic of early natural-isms to be anthropomorphic about nature than to apply concepts to man whose first application had been to inanimate nature; indeed there were few such concepts, for the microcosm–macrocosm ratio was more likely to begin with man than to end with him. When the organic, neo-Platonic, or Aristotelian conception of nature was surrendered and replaced by the corpuscular and mechanical one, there occurred the great bifurcation of nature by which man and his works were seen to be unnatural and to require a very different mode of understanding from that of nature. But the reaction against this humanistic bifurcation was swift; it is found especially in Hobbes and Spinoza, who tried to "consider human actions and desires in exactly the same manner as though [he] were concerned with lines, planes, and solids." The epigones of these great naturalistic philosophers in the next century, men like La Mettrie and d'Holbach, produced jejune philosophical systems as if the program had actually been accomplished; at the same time, patient work by men of science was persistently narrowing the gap between what might be true about man and what was ascertainably true about the rest of nature. While the major tradition in philosophy did not steadily adhere to this course and some of its most notable exemplars turned away from it, progress in science unremittingly reduced the scope and authority of man's claim to uniqueness and autonomy, the claim, already renounced by Spinoza, to be "situated in nature as a kingdom within a kingdom." The competing conceptions of man produced a crisis in the middle of the last century. This crisis passed, not because it was solved but because men learned to live with it or lost interest in it.

Recently, unprecedented advances in scientific understanding and technological power to change (or to end) life have reawakened the Victorian sense of insecurity. In desperate effort to preserve or reinstate the threatened uniqueness, freedom, and dignity of man, or to compromise the issue by re-anthropomorphizing nature, men have sought refuge in the foolishness of astrology, witchcraft, magic, and other forms of narcissism which most of us believed had been forever routed by science and philosophy.

Critics of the adequacy of the scientific model of man and scientific blueprints for his future must make a better stand than that, or else get on the bandwagon. In these lectures I want to examine and assess, as dispassionately as I can, the categorial structures of these two images of what man is and archetypes of what he can make himself and others into. I shall begin by examining the views held by those who compare human thinking to the operation of a machine and who conclude that the human brain is a "computer made of meat" and that man is a machine. The analogy between computer and brain is so startlingly good that there have been many investigations of the degree to which human actions like thinking can be replicated by and even should be attributed to machines. Thus arises the question "Can a machine think?" But my question is a slightly different one. It is: If human beings are machines, can *they* think? More specifically: If *I* am a machine, can *I* think?

In my question "Can a human machine think?" there are two words that require examination: "machine" and "think."

A machine in the literal sense of the word is an arrangement of matter devised so that a dependable correspondence is secured between controllable input and usable output. To say something is a machine is to say that there is some, presumably human, purpose which it serves and for which it was devised. If there are several links between controllable input and usable output, such correspondence is seldom if ever given to us in the ready-made constellations of matter we find in the world. Such correspondence must be devised by our setting up isolated systems in which the free play of the parts is restricted and their changes are determined by intentional human manipulations.

Energy is constantly raining on an automobile engine, and the engine is giving off energy in usable, useless, and even undesirable forms. But the controllable input of fuel regulated by the foot on the accelerator is correlated in dependable ways with the useful output of locomotion. The correlation of controllable inputs with useful outputs is, of course, never perfect and at best lies only within a range of tolerable variation. But an ideal machine may be defined as one about which, if we know the controllable input, we can accurately predict the usable output; alternatively, it is a machine whose output is precisely determined by controlling the input.

What I have said is as applicable to a computing machine as it is to a gasoline engine. In a computer the input and output energies are small, but they are highly articulated as signals. The input signals stand in no one-to-one correspondence to output signals, but groups of the former, together with signals already stored in the machine, are transformed into groups of the latter in rule-governed ways. The only reason that we cannot in fact predict the output of the computer is that the computer transforms these signals into printouts more rapidly than we can; it is the gap between the theoretical predictability and the actual unpredictability that makes computers useful.

In the literal sense of the word 'machine', a machine is devised for the accomplishment of a purpose. Without conscious beings, their objectives, and their techniques there would be no machines in the literal sense. But the word 'machine' is also applied metaphorically to some things not devised by human beings and things whose existence is independent of human purposes. It is in this sense that our ancestors compared the heavens to a clock and called them a machine. We do so now only to refer to the regularity of the behavior of the heavens, which is so uniform that, at least until very recently, it was the standard by which real clocks—machines in the literal sense—were tested. The machine metaphor began in a theological context, in an age in which the analogy of the solar system to a machine devised by human beings was felt to be much richer than it now is. The solar system was literally a machine to those who thought it was designed and constructed by God; for us, however, the solar system is a machine only in a metaphorical sense, since we drop all thought of design and intentional arrangement and have reference only to the predictability of motions that occur in it.

When we now speak of "the human machine" we post-Darwinians use the word 'machine' only in the metaphorical sense, whereas when we say that a computer is a machine, we are using the word in its literal sense. In the metaphor of "the human machine" we refer to the regularity of the behavior of the body as an instance of what would be expected from our knowledge of the laws of physics and chemistry, and we no longer explain the arrangements and functions of the organs of the body by recourse to any conscious purposes held by our Creator; we do not speak of purposes but only of physicochemical causes for the body's structure and function. When we compare the body to a chemical factory, we do not consider the fact that in a real chemical factory a distillation column is put in a particular place for the sake of a particular human purpose; we mean only that there is no process *in vivo* that cannot, in principle, be duplicated *in vitro*.

The word 'think' likewise has at least two meanings. It refers to a process and to an accomplishment. In the first sense, 'thinking' names something that goes on inside one's head, as it were, undiscerned by anyone but the man who is doing the thinking. I cannot define 'thinking' but at least for our purposes here it needs no definition; it is one of the things you and I are doing now, and each of us is aware that he *is* doing it now. It is distinguishable from feeling and daydreaming, since there are right and wrong ways of thinking but hardly right and wrong ways of feeling and daydreaming. Thinking has to do with the evaluation of evidence, the forming of conjectures or hypotheses, their evaluation, and deliberate choice between alternative solutions to problems. To think means to subject purposefully the stream of consciousness to logical rules, to try to keep it on the right track between evidence and conclusion.

'Thinking' in the second sense has reference to accomplishments we naively suppose can be achieved only by going through the process just described. Thinking, says Skinner, "does not explain overt behavior: it is simply more behavior to be explained. . . . Thinking is behaving. The mistake is in allocating the behavior to the mind." [1] It is in this sense that we say to a man who has made a silly mistake, "You are not thinking." We do not mean that he was unconscious; we do not even mean that he was not engaged in a process that he might candidly describe as thinking in

1. *About Behaviorism* (New York, 1974), p. 104. See Wittgenstein, *Philosophical Investigations* (Oxford, 1963), §§330–32; G. Ryle, *The Concept of Mind* (New York, 1949), p. 283.

the first sense. We mean merely that he did not get the answer right when he could have and should have got it right. He may sincerely respond to our censure that he surely was thinking; but in so doing, he retreats from the second meaning of the word back to the first. And if he says that he was thinking in the first sense of the word, we are not in a position to gainsay him, except to reply that he was not thinking very well.

In the question "Can a human machine think?" we are using the word 'machine' in the metaphorical sense. In the question "Can a computing machine think?" we are using the word 'machine' in the literal sense and the word 'think' in the first of the two senses. In each of the questions, we assume that both can think in the second of the two senses and query whether they can think also in the first of the two senses. While it may seem obvious that the human being, even if it is a machine in the metaphorical sense, can think, it is not obvious that the computing machine, a machine in the literal sense, can think in the first sense even if we concede that it can think in the second sense.

If we did not believe that there is good reason to say that the literal machine can think in the second sense, no question as to whether it can think in the first sense would ever have arisen. But while it seems obvious that human beings, whether metaphorically machines or not, can think in sense one, it is hard to believe that what is literally a machine can think in sense one, because we know how to explain the public signs of its thinking (thinking in sense two) without having recourse to saying, as we do in the case of men, that it is thinking in sense one. We understand the circuitry by which controllable input information is converted into usable output information, and there is no place in such explanation for appeals to conscious thought on the part of the transistors and relays that make up the machine. We do not know enough neurology, however, to dispense with thinking in sense one in our explanation of thinking in sense two when we are dealing with a human being and trying to understand him as a machine even in the metaphorical sense.

Still, it is hard to see why we need to draw a sharp distinction between what we attribute to a literal machine and what we attribute to other men in the way of thinking. In cases of thinking in sense two by other men do we not always have recourse to the hypothesis that they were thinking also in sense one? But maybe if we knew as much neurology as we do electronics we should never have recourse to thinking in sense one as something going on in another person. All my evidence that either other men or machines think is that they get right answers which I can get only by going through a process of thinking in sense one. I lack direct inspectable evidence that other men think in sense one just as I lack evidence that machines think in sense one. Conversely, any hypothesis that other men think in sense one because they think in sense two would be in principle justified in the case of machines also.

That we have the same kind of evidence that machines and men think has often been denied in the past, when the accomplishments of machines in thinking in sense two were much less impressive than they are today. We may smile superciliously at Descartes' argument that evidence that men are not automata is to be found in the fact that men, unlike machines, can not only answer questions but can also engage in rational discourse. But any argument that a machine cannot do some specified task which men can do is likely to be refuted by the invention of a machine that *can* do it. I do not wish to base any argument on this premise of surplus human accomplishment, for the surplus is not only continuously decreasing; it may indeed become a deficit, since there are many tasks of thinking in sense two that a machine can do better than a man.

I will take for granted, for the sake of getting on to my own argument, that any human thinking in sense two can be at least matched by a future machine. I assume that the rule-governed conversion of input information to output information, where there is a clear distinction between following and breaking a rule, is capable of being programmed into a machine, so that there is no question susceptible of being answered with a demonstrably right answer by a human being that cannot also be answered by a machine. And I assume that problems whose solution cannot be reached by rigid adherence to a program-mable algorism may be solved by a machine with randomized or probabilistic programs at least about as well as they are solved by men. These assumptions may be unwarranted or false, but that is no matter; they play no part in my argument and are made merely to dissociate my argument from others designed to show that, since men can think better than machines, they cannot be machines.[2]

I propose now to try to show that if human beings are machines, no argument suffices to show that they are. It may be the case that human beings are machines, either literally or metaphorically. I propose to prove only that there can be no conclusive argument to show that they are. On the other hand, if human beings are not machines, at least plausible arguments can be given to show that they *are* machines. There is the following paradox: If the machine theory is true, we cannot rationally argue for it. If it is false, however, we can rationally (but not, of course, correctly) argue for it. The machine theory is self-stultifying.

Self-stultification is not a fallacy of formal logic. There is nothing self-contradictory in the statement "I am a machine." Arguments of impeccable formal validity and with much empirical support can be formulated with this as their conclusion.

A card-shuffling machine rearranging cards with sentences printed on them can produce fortuitous

2. These assumptions have been sharply challenged by Hubert Dreyfus in his book *What Computers Can't Do* (New York, 1972). But since my argument is very different from his, though with a like conclusion, I wish to dissociate it from his by assuming what he rejects and then to show that there is still something computers can't do. Actually it makes no difference to my argument whether the truth lies with these assumptions or with Dreyfus' attack on them, but my argument will appear more distinctive and less vulnerable to (in fact irrelevant) objections if the Dreyfus line of argument is set aside at once. That is my purpose in making these assumptions.

arrangements of cards that state valid and sound arguments. Naturally, a card-shuffling machine produces many more sequences that will not even read like arguments and others that look like arguments but are neither sound nor valid. But if a machine can, even accidentally, produce sound arguments, then obviously a human organism that is a machine can do so also.

The thesis that the machine theory is self-stultifying is left untouched by this consideration, because self-stultifying does not mean invalid, or never producing, or being incapable of producing, a sound argument. Rather, it means that the conditions under which an argument is taken as contributing to the proof of a conclusion are incompatible with the conditions that explain why the conclusion was drawn. In every case, whether the machine theory is correct or not, the conditions under which an argument is taken as proof are different from the conditions that produced it. The former belong to the realm of logic and evidence; the latter belong to psychology and physiology or (if the machine theory is correct) to physics and chemistry. A process of thinking in the second sense, whether by a machine or a man, can apparently be explained in terms of either set of conditions. We avail ourselves of the one when we are making, recognizing, and evaluating an argument, of the other when we are citing the causes why it was given.

Difference of conditions does not imply incompatibility of conditions. To define what is meant here by 'incompatibility,' I must first define another term, 'probative value.' An argument has probative value if it constitutes, in the mind of a rational man, a ground for credence in the conclusion of the argument. An argument lacks probative value if it does not increase the rational credibility of its conclusion. An interesting argument (e.g., one not in the form p ⊃ p) discovered to be sound (premisses known to be true, inference known to be valid) is maximally probative. If a man knows that an argument is sound, he cannot ask for a more decisive or persuasive reason why he should accept its conclusion; he already knows all he needs to know in order to be sure that the conclusion is true. If T and T′ are true premisses and known to be true, there is no other true proposition U that, conjoined with T and T″, will increase (or decrease) the rational credibility of the deductive conclusion from T and T′. Any other proposition U that would decrease it would be known to be inconsistent with T or T′ and would therefore be known to be false. On the other hand, an argument known to be unsound has no probative value, even if its conclusion should be in fact true and believed to be true.

But often we do not enjoy the luxury of knowing whether all our premisses are true. While we can tell that an argument is valid because we have in logic definite tests of validity, we generally only believe that our premisses are true. We may believe them on evidence sufficient for a rational man; but the rational man may have sufficient evidence for believing a conclusion and may rationally believe it when, as a matter of fact, it is false. Now a valid argument from rationally believed premisses T and T′ may not be known to be sound and may not in fact be sound and yet may have probative value in that it raises the rational credibility of the conclusion C. It would be irrational to accept T and T' and not accept C; and if one had previously doubted C, the argument from T and T' to C would have probative value in that it would raise the credibility of C in the eyes of the rational man who had accepted T and T'.

In the case of a sound deductive argument, there is no proposition U that, added to the premises, can make the argument unsound. But in the case of an argument of less than maximum probative value (i.e., an argument not known to be sound), there can be some proposition U known or believed to be true that when added to T and T' reduces the probative value of the argument. A proposition U that has this power is said to be incompatible with the argument from T and T' to C, but need not be logically inconsistent with the premises T and T'.

To illustrate: a rational man might know or believe that the person who gives him the argument "T and T' imply C, so you ought to accept C" is his enemy, who is anxious to trap him. The proposition U, namely, "The proponent of this argument is my enemy," added to the argument does not affect its validity and its soundness (if it is valid and sound), but it may properly reduce the credence the rational hearer of the argument accords to the conclusion.

This is a case of mere incompatibility. But if the proposition that is incompatible with the argument is a corollary of the conclusion itself, the argument is self-stultifying. Any argument used by Epimenides to support his conclusion "All Cretans are liars" would be self-stultifying because the conclusion (especially if true) reduces the probative value of the argument that led to it.

It is my thesis that: (1) no one knows the machine theory to be true and no one knows whether there is a sound argument that proves it; (2) for any argument in its favor there is a proposition U that reduces its probative value; (3) the proposition that does so is a corollary of the machine theory itself, and any argument for the machine theory is therefore self-stultifying.

Let us suppose that I am presented with a valid argument in favor of a certain theory, which has plausible premisses. If I believe the argument is presented by a rational man who found the premisses credible to him the argument has more probative value to me than if I believe it was generated by a card-shuffling machine. In either case, of course, I have to evaluate the argument and make my own decision about it, but the argument of a rational man comes to me with some credential lacking in the argument produced by a card-shuffling machine whose input was items from the daily newspaper.

According to the machine theory of the behavior of a man, what he utters he utters because of his brain state, which is exclusively determined by antecedent physiological conditions, and an argument from a rational man has an antecedent credential based only on induction. We find that some men, unlike card-shuffling machines, regularly produce sound arguments, and we call men who do so "rational." No one who holds that human beings are mere robots has ever held that there is no difference (physiological) as evidenced in thinking in sense two between rational and irrational men; and no one has argued that men are like card-shuffling machines. That a card-shuffling machine produces arguments without antecedent probative value does not show that a brain-machine cannot produce arguments that do have probative value. And a fortiori since an IBM machine can produce arguments of high probative value, obviously a brain, even if it be only a machine, can do so. Hence the derogatory things I have said about card-shuffling machines cannot be carried over into a distrust of all machine-produced or brain-produced arguments.

There may be, however, an important difference between arguments produced by machines and arguments produced by rational men, a difference that should not be obscured by the fact that we decide that a man is rational in much the same way that we decide that an IBM machine is a good data-processor and a card-shuffling machine is not; namely, by keeping score on successes and failures.

Where does the IBM machine fall in the gradient between the silly card-shuffling machine and an intelligent man? Surely, in one respect, close to the rational man; the machine's successes are at the very least comparable to the man's successes. But in another respect the IBM machine is closer to the card-shuffling machine in that its printout is categorially more comparable to the card-shuffling machine's sequences than it is to a man's arguments and answers. If we suppose all three—card-shuffling machine, IBM machine, and man—are giving arguments or answers to questions, the IBM machine and the man are in one class and the card-shuffling machine in another. But if we ask what the three things are doing—giving answers or doing something quite different—then the card-shuffling machine and the IBM belong together, and the man is in a class by himself. We must raise the question as to what we mean by a "machine-produced answer" in contrast to a "man-produced answer" quite independently of the question as to whether induction teaches that the former may be the "right answer" just as often as the latter may. Is there a single genus, "answer," with two species, "machine-produced" and "man-produced," or are there two quite different things—printout and discourse—called by the same name because of some structural characteristics they share?

As the words "argument" and "answer" are ordinarily used, they refer to the execution of an intention that is achieved by a rule-governed process in which a "right answer" or "correct argument" is given because it is seen to be right or correct. "Right" and "correct" are not just terms used in the evaluation of an argument; they are terms built into the meaning of "answer" and "argument," not in the sense that every answer is right and every argument correct but in the sense that unless there is normally an intention to give the right answer or a correct argument, the terms "answering" and "arguing" lose their meaning. A parrot trained to utter the sound "y-e-s" to any stimulus-sentence with a rising inflexion cannot be said to "give an answer" to the question: "Are you a parrot?" Its response, though it sounds like a true answer, is not an answer at all, since it is stimulus-determined, not rule-governed, and lacks probative value.

The rule-governed process of answering a question, or a process isomorphic with the rule-governed process of thinking in sense one, can be replicated by a machine in the literal sense of the word; namely, by an arrangement of matter devised by a human being for the express purpose of replicating the human processes leading to thinking in sense two.

But the output of machines in the literal sense is "answers" and "arguments" only in a parasitic sense. They are seen to be answers only when we compare the output to what we could, in principle, produce as the expression of thinking in sense one, where considerations of appropriateness, validity, and evidence are taken into account in the conduct of the thinking. Such considerations are unintelligible except in a context containing, or thought to contain, thinking in sense one and would not be intelligible in the vocabulary restricted to outward behavior, which is called thinking (in sense two) only because we embed it in a context of thinking in sense one. When we call an utterance an "answer," and even more when we say it is correct, we are ratifying it as conforming to standards we understand only because we know what it is to think in sense one; we ratify it because it conforms to the intentions and rules that guide thinking in sense one to its outward expression as thinking in sense two.

"Rational explanations," writes J. R. Lucas,[3] "are two-faced. They give the reasons why *I did* the action in question, but also the reasons why *one should*." An explanation given by or of a machine is not two-faced.

An explanation of the behavior of a machine takes the following form. Let S_1 stand for the state of affairs at time t_1 and S_2 for the state of affairs at t_2, the state-descriptions being independent of each other and belonging to physics and chemistry. Let L be the covering physical or chemical law with variables for S_1 and S_2, and let "$\rightarrow$" mean "implies." Then an explanation of why the machine is in state S_2 at t_2 is

$$(1)\ S_1 L \rightarrow S_2$$

Now suppose S_1 and S_2 describe states of a computing machine in terms of which relays are open and which are shut. S_1 describes the state that results from input expressing the proposition $T \cdot T'$, and S_2 describes the state that results in the output expressed by the proposition C. L will contain, in addition to physical laws, also the program so arranged that S_1 is followed by S_2 if and only if

$$(2)\ T \cdot T' \rightarrow C$$

But it is not the case that $S_1 \rightarrow S_2$. For that implication to hold, L must also be true (the physical laws in it must be true, and the program must be effective). Nor is it the case that $(2) \rightarrow L$. L is at best an empirical truth (the physical laws in L are empirically true, and it is empirically true that the machine follows the

3. *The Freedom of the Will* (Oxford, 1970), p. 42.

program). Hence (1) does not have the probative value for C that (2) does, though (1) tells the whole truth about why the machine printed C. The same explanation mutatis mutandis would be given had the machine printed C even if (2) were false.

The machine, of course, is not telling us why it printed C, and a fortiori does not give us reasons why *"one should"* conclude C given T and T'. It is we who explain the machine's behavior by adducing (1), and we can do this regardless of whether (2) is true or false, known or unknown to us. If we did not previously know (1) but are convinced that the machine's print-out is correct, so that we accord it probative value, this is because of our belief in the empirical proposition that the program has been so devised that the machine will print C only if (2) is true. But this can be known inductively, if at all.

When we speak in a commonsense way of a person and answer the question "Why did he assert C?" we may give one or more of the following answers: "C is the correct answer," "He believed C to be the correct answer," or "He is intelligent and honest, and usually says what he thinks." The first of these answers accords with formula (2), and the second and third are analogous to the explanation of a machine's behavior given by formula (1). But if the machine theory of the human person is correct, then it is just as if we were talking about an IBM machine that has printed "C," and the answer that falls under formula (2) is irrelevant; the machine would have printed and the man would have said "C" under the conditions of formula (1) regardless of whether (2) was correct or not.

In the explanation of machine behavior we make use of formula (2), if at all, only indirectly, by our knowing that the IBM engineers who designed the machine knew formula (2) and by our knowing that they devised the machine so that it would print C only when the input was T and T'. Once the machine builds up a good reputation by telling us what we do know, we may trust it to tell us what we do not know. But the explanation of the machine's behavior is found solely by referring to formula (1); the reason why *one should* accept C as the answer has been put into the machine by a human thinker for whom formula (2) is a rule but not a descriptive law.

But if the designer of the machine is himself a machine whose states are beliefs connected by causal laws, then the truth of T and T' is not the reason for belief C, but the belief in T and T' causes the belief C. A human being about whom this proposition is true is a machine, but, in Leibniz's terminology, an *automaton spirituale*.

Let us identify (in some sense, either directly or indirectly, contingently or necessarily) the belief in $T \cdot T'$ with the state S_1 and the belief in C with S_2 in formula (1). L is a set of irreducible psychological laws and a program established by education. It will then be possible by citing only (1) to explain why a person who believes $T \cdot T'$ goes through a process called thinking and comes to believe C. Such an answer calls attention to the contingent fact that a person like him will ceteris paribus believe C. But his belief in C and the explanation of his belief in C under formula (1) now constitute no reason why *one should* believe C; the only reason why one should believe C is given in formula (2).

If C is "The machine theory is true," the argument which led to it even when expressed in mentalistic language of belief is self-stultifying because (1), which is a corollary of the machine theory, is not a good reason that *one should* have for believing C. It is only an inductive explanation (since (1) is empirical) of why someone else does believe it. While it is a very good explanation of that, it is not a reason why *I should* believe it.

The argument just given, that the machine theory is self-stultifying, has a peculiar limitation. It is self-stultifying only when I claim it to be the truth about all men or about me alone. But it is certainly an odd theory that holds that the statement "Men are machines" may be true of all men except the man who gives good reasons for accepting it. Yet whatever plausibility the machine theory has—and it has much plausibility and is a rich model for psychology and neurology—it gains by being associated with a self-exemption clause.

There is no obvious self-stultification in my argument that you and all the rest of mankind are complicated on-line computers. But I cannot, without self-stultification, argue or accept an argument that my own thinking is merely an epiphenomenon of a process the whole truth about which is given in a causal formula that states its sufficient condition.

There is a class of sentences that are intrinsically useless because one cannot imagine a situation in which they could be used. Some examples are: "I am sicker than I think I am," and "I believe it is raining but it is not." These sentences are not formally self-contradictory because their equivalents spoken by another person (for example, "Beck is sicker than he thinks he is") are possibly true. But any argument *I* gave in support of any of them would be obviously self-stultifying or pragmatically self-defeating.

"I am a machine" is such a sentence, and any argument that would plausibly lead *you* to believe it of me can have no probative value for me. The premisses of your argument, which imply this conclusion, could lead me to say or believe "I am a machine" only through the mechanism that makes my acceptance of the "conclusion" relate to my acceptance of the "premisses" contingently through an empirical law. I might in some fashion be persuaded to believe it, but I could not be rationally convinced of it. I have no reason for believing it if I believe it only because (causally because) my belief is an effect of other beliefs. If the machine theory is true and I believe it, I do so only by virtue of a contingent law of my behavior. If, however, it is false and I believe it, I may do so for good reasons and not because I causally must.

Even if I thus succeed in establishing the nullity of the argument that I am a machine, I have done nothing to rescue you from the demeaning fate of being machines. Presumably, however, each of you could formulate exactly the same argument with respect to yourself. The argument made by you, in turn, would leave me in the same situation in which my argument left you. My argument that I am not a machine could have no weight with you, because everything I am heard by you to say could be said by a talking machine instead of by a thinking person. But if you adapt my argument to your position and if each of us uses it for himself, then each of us will know himself to be other than a machine, though each of us will know it only of himself.

I wish to use the word "solipsism" in a sense slightly different from the one that is perhaps usual. Usually, I believe, it denotes the denial that there is any other center of consciousness than I. Consciousness, however, while no doubt essential to selfhood, seems to me to be less relevant here than one of its corollaries. The machine theory need not necessarily deny that some machines are conscious; consciousness might well be an epiphenomenon of thinking in sense two. However ubiquitous consciousness might be, if the machine theory is true it is, in Lovejoy's happy phrase, not a part of "the executive order of nature." A person who asserts that men are machines but exempts himself from this generalization in order to avoid stultifying his own argument is, as I wish to use the word, a solipsist.

Many jokes have been made about putative solipsists, as if they could be laughed out of their folly; someone told Bertrand Russell how sorry he was that there were not as many solipsists as there used to be. But laughing a philosopher out of his folly is not as good a tactic as refuting his thesis. This, however, cannot be done by any straightforward argument ad rem.

I am bound to lose any such argument I have with a

solipsist, since he can discount any argument I might give. It is in vain, therefore, to argue directly against a solipsist, for the solipsist position is impregnable since it always permits this discount. Even if solipsism is false, the solipsist is invulnerable to counter-solipsist arguments.

Only A. C. Ewing,[4] I think, has indicated a possible transcendental argument against solipsism. He said, "If solipsism is true, there are no solipsists, since I am not one." This short way with solipsism, almost a throwaway that Ewing consigned to a footnote, seems to me to be profoundly important.

The solipsist position has never been maintained if it is true, because if it is true I alone could have maintained it, and I have not done so. If I argued for solipsism—it is hard to see why I should do so even if, or especially if, I believed it—I could not do so in good faith, because I do not believe it. If I were to choose to argue that it is true, my position would be invulnerable to counterargument even if it is false. But I do not choose to do so.

I freely and without mental reservations of any kind solemnly affirm and swear: I am not now, nor have I ever been, a solipsist. I believe I live in a world with other human beings who are, on the whole, like me.

I believe this argument, invented by Ewing, is likewise usable by others and is not discountable when extended to others. This argument will carry no weight, of course, with another person if he is a genuine solipsist who knows his business. But if there is

4. *Idealism: A Critical Survey* (London, 1934), p. 242 n.

such a person, I know that solipsism is false since that person is not I.

The first argument in this lecture was perhaps discourteous since it left you, so far as I know, unthinking machines. The second argument makes amends for this in my uncoerced acknowledgment of you as thinking beings. You could accept the first of the arguments and leave me out; but I ask the same courtesy of you that my second argument extends to you. If you believe you are not a machine but that I am, I do not know why you are reading this book. C. D. Broad[5] once said, "If I hear a man refer to his brother or his house-cat as an 'interesting mechanism', I know he is either a fool or a physiologist." We, neither fools nor physiologists, have serious philosophical work to do together.

5. Regrettably, I cannot find the passage where Broad said this. One expects in vain to find it on pp. 5 or 624 of *The Mind and its Place in Nature* (London, 1925). But it sounds broadly authentic.

2: ACTORS AND SPECTATORS

When we, neither fools nor physiologists, acknowledge each other's existence as thinking beings, we do not ipso facto regard each other as alike in all respects. There are men I regard as more intelligent than I am, others as less intelligent; there are many empirical differences between us. But there is one simple and universal distinction between me and everyone else. I *think* I know myself better than I know you, and in a different way. Though I can observe myself and be a spectator of what I am doing, ordinarily I just act and, without having to perform a second act of self-observation, know what I am doing. The business of acting is very different from the specific business of observing. I can know what you are doing only by acting in one specific way, namely observing and interpreting your actions which I do not "just know." I can cooperate with you, try to guide your actions, or protect myself from them. But the first thing I must do is notice or observe them.

It will be well to introduce some terminological distinctions so that I do not have to talk repeatedly about you and me. We are all persons (etymologically: masked actors). A person acts, and as a being which acts he is an *agent*. One of the acts that a person does is to observe and try to explain the acts of a person, usually another person. An agent who does this is called a *spectator*. The agent whom he observes is, vis-à-vis the spectator, called the *actor*. (While it will be important and easy to maintain the distinction between actor and spectator, it will sometimes be neither important nor easy to maintain the verbal distinction

33

between actor and agent, and when it is awkward to do so I will ignore it.)

Each of us is an agent, but there are no spectators without actors, no actors without spectators. 'Agent' is an ontological term, 'actor' and 'spectator' are perspectival or histrionic terms. 'Agent' and 'actor' may refer to the same person, just as "Mary Doe" may have the same denotation as "Mrs. John Doe"; yet there are statements we are justified in making about the woman according to which name is used in the context. For example, "Mary Doe married John Doe" is synthetic, while "Mrs. John Doe is the wife or widow of John Doe" is analytic. Analogously, there may be things said about the actor that cannot be said about the agent, and vice versa.

Calling an agent an "actor" raises the question "Actor for what spectator?" This question may sometimes be trivial, but it is important if the information the spectator reports is determined by *his* interests and presuppositions when these are different from the interests and presuppositions of other spectators and of the agent who is doing the observed action.

I can be a spectator of you and see you as a machine, as a *homo economicus,* as a member of Yale University, as a man or a woman, as a friend. Some of these roles are largely determined by you, your situation, and how you regard yourself; that is, what you observe yourself *as.* Others are largely or exclusively determined by me. There can thus arise a clash between roles assumed by agents and roles assigned by spectators. Suppose I am a fool or physiologist and see you as "an interesting mechanism." Then almost everything I say about you as actor will be rejected by you as agent, because if my earlier argument is valid you cannot regard these spectator statements about you as the truth.

A difference between the agent in propria persona and the agent as actor can be vividly brought out by a simple comparison between what is permitted to a spectator of my actions and what I as an agent may do. I cannot meaningfully say: "I believe it is raining, but it is not." But you can say, "Beck believes it is raining, but it is not." In saying I believe it is raining, I am avowing a belief, but in the second clause I take back what I avowed in the first. What I have said is not a formal contradiction, because the second sentence, "Beck believes it is raining, but it is not," reports the same facts and is not self-contradictory but may indeed be true. I cannot have a good reason to say what you may have a good reason to say, even though we are saying the same thing.

Some significant differences between what an agent can say and what a spectator can say about him emerge from this little example. First, expressions like "I believe" and "I know" carry a commitment by the person who says them which is not made by the spectator, and what follows the spectator's act of referring to the agent's beliefs (what else the spectator says) may be very different from what follows from the agent's act of expressing the belief. "I believe" determines the truth-value I impute to the proposition that follows it; "Beck believes" does not determine it for the speaker of that sentence. Second (at least in this example), the spectator must know *more* than the agent. He must not only know that the agent believes it is raining but he must know (or claim to know) that the agent is wrong. Third, the agent may know something better than the spectator knows it, for instance, whether he genuinely believes that it is raining or is lying when he says "I believe it is raining." The spectator often cannot be sure about this, and when he is sure about it the procedure for getting this assurance is very different from the way in which the agent knows it; in fact, normally the agent has no way of getting to know it at all but just knows it, while the spectator may have to be a detective using a polygraph to reach his conclusion about it.

There is thus an asymmetry in the actor–spectator confrontation. Philosophers cannot but be interested in this asymmetry. It is intrinsically important as an aspect of the problem of philosophical anthropology, which is to answer the question "What is man?" Is this to be answered in the language and within the framework of spectator or of agent? And if the spectator's answer is to be accepted, which spectator is to be preferred, the self-spectator or the other-spectator? The physiologically oriented spectator or the sociological? If the answers from these perspectives are necessarily different, how can they be brought together if they are complementary or reconciled if they are inconsistent? But the problem is not one merely of philosophical anthropology; it lies close to the epistemological roots of the social sciences, from which the social sciences grow out into two trunks: the theory and corpus of reports on how human agents appear as actors to spectators who act to achieve objective and anonymous observation of actors; and the institution of social science itself, which regulates those agents called spectators, whose principal act is observing and explaining the actions of others. The problem has a poignancy lacking in many intellectual concerns. One does not have to be a romantic misfit sometimes to feel with despair that "nobody understands"; nor an obscurantist enemy of scientism to feel that advances in computer technology and neurophysiology somehow constitute a threat to the autonomy of oneself as agent; nor in love with another person sometimes to feel frustrated in the vain effort to leave one's own unique existential individuality behind and to see the world as someone else does. We are dealing here with problems of knowing ourselves and each other, and these problems are pervasive in life whether we are philosophers, psychologists, anthropologists, or just plain people.

I shall now present the script of a little drama. I shall be the angel in two senses: the man who sponsors the performance, and the one who occupies, in Samuel Alexander's apt terminology, "the angel's point of view," [1] who omnisciently knows what is really going on both backstage and onstage. Do not ask me how I know it; I will appear in the third act (chapter 4) not as a deus ex machina, but as an ordinary actor.

Our cast of characters consists of three persons: a child, another person of ordinary but not extraordinary sensitivity, and a "fool or physiologist." Each is

1. Used, though for another purpose, in *Space, Time and Deity* (London, 1920), 1:19–20.

allowed to tell his own story about the child. The child is agent. The first man, whom we call Spectator I, gives a commonsense description and explanation of the child's behavior. The second man makes his description and explanation of the child's behavior conform to the categories that he would apply in describing and explaining the behavior of a rat or a machine in his laboratory. We call him Spectator II.

Upon hearing the angelic voice ask "What is going on here?" each of the three makes his own answer.

The child responds, "I am doing my homework, which must be handed in tomorrow, but I can't seem to get this problem right."

The first spectator answers, "The child is doing his homework, which must be handed in tomorrow, and is angry because he cannot work a problem."

The second spectator answers: "From 9:01 to 9:02 the child sat at a table, holding a pen in his right hand. He made marks on the paper four times. He scratched his head with his left hand at 9:01:26. He threw down his pen at 9:01:50."

The first two answers are substantially identical but differ markedly from the third. The first two contain teleological terms ("doing" something) and make reference to a rule (homework must be correct and turned in on time). The third does not make any mention of rules by reference to which the behavior of the child can be judged as successful or not. To be sure, Spectator II almost says, or at least allows us to infer, why the child did some of the things he did; he scratched his head presumably because it itched, and he held the pen in order to write. "Scratch" and "hold" are words that refer to actions done with a purpose, but so minimally that they could be used even in describing what a machine does, as in "This bolt holds the lever in place." Even these minimally teleological words like "making a mark," "holding the pen," and "scratching his head" could be replaced by expressions that name what is observed without explanatory overtones. Spectator II could, and if he wants to be a physiologist and nothing more probably should, describe the child's holding the pen by referring only to geometrical and physical relations between specific muscles, bones, and a small plastic cylinder positioned between three bones. This replacement of words, however, is not translation, not just saying the same thing in a different way, as Skinner believes to be possible at least in principle.[2] There are many ways of doing the same action, using sometimes this set of muscles, sometimes that. On a specific occasion when Spectator I says the child is writing, Spectator II says muscles 71, 83, and 99 behave in such and such a manner. If this were a translation of what the first spectator says, there would be a rule for its production from what the first spectator says, and this rule could be followed again and again. But it cannot be; the next time the one says "the child is writing," the other cannot just look up this rule of translation; he must look at the child again, and he may find that a

2. He says, "No doubt many of the mentalistic expressions embedded in the English language cannot be as rigorously translated as 'sunrise', but acceptable translations are not out of reach." *Beyond Freedom and Dignity* (New York, 1971), p. 24. See also *About Behaviorism* (New York, 1974), p. 95.

different set of muscles is involved this time. He would then have to describe in other terms what Spectator I described in the same terms, and the description by one of them is therefore not a translation of the description by the other. Each says a different thing, not the same thing in a different way.

Indeed there are many statements by the first spectator which cannot even apparently be translated into language appropriate to the second. For instance, since the first two reports are about what the child is doing in the sense of what he is trying to accomplish, the first spectator can ask the child, "Have you finished it yet? Did you get it right?" But the second spectator cannot ask such a question, for to him there is no "it" that was to be finished or got right, but just one movement after another. The word "it" does not stand for something like, but not identical with, anything that Spectator II saw; it is not an item he just failed to see but could have seen had he looked closer. "It" is of a different logical type from reflexes, hand movements, and muscular contractions; "it" refers to the action the child is performing, not to an item in the behavior but to the unity of the behavior, the theme that ties the writing and the head-scratching and the angry gesture into a story that makes sense.

The first pair of answers about what the child is doing is independent of the third. If the child had been standing and writing with a pencil, answers 1 and 2 might remain exactly the same, but answer 3 would be totally different. The third answer is in turn independent of the answers in the first pair. The third answer might be exactly the same, while the answer given by the child and the other spectator could have been "I am working a puzzle" or "The child is pretending to work."

There is some dependence between answers of the two types, however, inasmuch as some possible answers of the first type are incompatible with some possible answers of the second type.[3] The first spectator's answer does not entail what Spectator II *will* say, but it does exclude some answers Spectator II *might* give because they would be false, and some things Spectator II might truly say would indicate that some answers by Spectator I would have to be false. If Spectator II truly said, "The child is asleep," "The child is running," or "The child's heart is not beating," then "The child is doing his homework" would be false. Any statement by

3. We can, of course, find simpler cases in which the descriptions by Spectators I and II would strongly suggest each other to a third spectator who could understand both. For example, Spectator I could say that the child is whistling, and Spectator II could describe the way his mouth and diaphragm are functioning; it is not far-fetched to say that he is whistling if and only if his mouth and diaphragm are doing precisely what they are found to be doing when, on one occasion, the child is said to be whistling. But if the child is whistling for his dog or trying to whistle a tune but getting it a little bit wrong, the one-to-one correspondence is hopelessly lost. If the answer by Spectator II is made more elaborate and includes references to (unobserved) brain-states that are presumably different and contingent upon what the child is concerned with, or if the first and second answers are made simpler and less specific, as, for example, "making marks on paper," we might expect eventually to get to answers of types 1 and 2 and answers of type 3 that are not independent of each other. Unless the child will be content to answer something like "I am moving my finger" and Spectator II can include enough brain physiology in his report to distinguish between the case of the child's moving his finger and his finger's moving, such parallelism and translatability between action reports and behavior reports cannot be expected.

the child or by Spectator I about what the child is doing implies the truth in answers by Spectator II that the child is living and showing behavior characteristic of a living organism, but beyond that hardly informative inference we cannot be much more specific. That the child is studying entails the falsity of the judgment that the child is having a fit, but not that muscle 73 instead of 74 is contracting or any manageably short series of such statements.

We shall call the events mentioned by Spectator II *behaviors* or *behavioral events,* and we shall say that two or more behavioral events are *functionally equivalent* if the replacement of one by the other in Spectator II's true answer does not affect the truth of the other two answers. Thus "hitting the keys of a typewriter" is a different behavioral event from "making marks with a pen," but they are functionally equivalent in that the replacement of one by the other in Spectator II's answer does not affect the truth of the other answers, that the child is writing his homework. Other true answers by the child or the other spectator, of course, may be affected; if they had answered that the child was typing his lesson, the other finger movements described by Spectator II would no longer be functionally equivalent. But answers by the agent and Spectator I are seldom so fine-grained that all alternative behaviorally equivalent events are excluded. The child might give boring detail about what he is doing, but would hardly change his story if Spectator II told him that he moved his hand from the wrist and not from the shoulder, and hence "moving hand from wrist" and "moving hand from shoulder" would be, even for this longer story, behaviorally equivalent.

Answers by the child and by the first spectator entail only a finite (though immensely large and somewhat vague) set of alternative descriptions by the second spectator, and no *one* of these alternative descriptions by the second spectator entails a specific answer by the child or the other spectator. At best only an immensely long conjunction of disjunctions of behavioral equivalents, most of which cannot be observed, in the second spectator's answer could say the same thing as "The child is preparing his homework."

The child's and the first spectator's answers determine, at least vaguely, the range of functionally equivalent behaviors. Unless Spectator II, by accepting the answer given by Spectator I, knows what is going on, he has no use for the concept of functionally equivalent behaviors; behavioral events are functionally equivalent *only* for the action as reported by the other spectator or the child. Behaviors may have no functional equivalents, either because there is only one way of performing the act in question (for example, there is perhaps only one way of responding affirmatively to the physician's request "Please cough") or because there is no known function that the specific behavior has in the performance of the act reported by the child or the other spectator. Behaviors of this kind being irrelevant to the act mentioned by Spectator I, no inferences concerning their occurrence can be drawn from his knowledge of the act. They have no functional equivalents, not because there is no other behavioral event that would have served just as well, but because they do nothing at all in the performance of the act. Only the kind of knowledge the child and the first spectator have can furnish the criteria of relevance and functional equivalence in the behavioral inventory made by the second spectator.

There is, of course, no guarantee that the child and the first spectator will recognize the same functional equivalents and draw the same lines between relevant and irrelevant behaviors, because the child and the first spectator might not agree on what the child is doing. Had Spectator I thought the child was acting to impress his parents, he might have noticed the deep frown on the child's face and interpreted it both as relevant and as functionally equivalent to an audible sigh. There is no single "standard description" that will determine, once and for all, what are relevant and equivalent behaviors. Perhaps not even the child's unavowed assessment of what he is doing, and certainly not what the child *says* he is doing, is a standard by which all spectators' reports are to be judged and corrected. Answers to the question "What is the child doing?" are never spectator-neutral and incorrigible.

The kind of questions the two spectators can ask and the child can answer will be different. Spectator I might show that he knows what is going on by asking, "Why are you writing with a pen?", and the child can answer, "The teacher requires it." Spectator II might ask, "Why did you scratch your head?", and the child might reply, "I don't know; I didn't even know I did it." The first spectator's question means: for what reason are you writing with a pen? The child's answer

will allude to his intention or to a rule that regulates
the action of doing homework. The second spectator's
question means: what caused you (or what made you)
scratch your head, or what are the circumstances
under which you usually or invariably scratch your
head, and which obtained at 9:01:26? And the child is
so unlikely to know the answer to that question that
Spectator II would hardly ask it of him, because he
thinks he can find the answer to that question without
the child's help.

Let us now put these remarks into summary form.

1. The agent knows what he is doing in the sense of
what he means to accomplish by his action. He knows
what his purpose is, or if he is not explicitly conscious
of his purpose he can, when asked, give an answer
without first considering what behavioral events are
taking place and then finding a hypothesis about his
motive and intention that explains them. On the other
hand, he may not know what he is doing in the sense of
what behavioral events are occurring. Out of the
ongoing stream of behavioral events that involve every
muscle in his body at every moment there are some few
of which he is aware as constituting the action that he
says he is doing. There are actions, like adding and
subtracting, that are ingredient in the action of solving
a problem he knows he is performing, and there may
be behavioral events made actions by his setting
himself to do *them*, for example, closing his fingers
around the pen.

The agent reports his actions in the first-person
form; the only proper subject of an action-verb is
personal, whereas behavioral event-verbs may have

(some do, some do not) other subjects, such as "My hand trembled," and "I didn't wink at the girl, my eye twitched." Normally the agent is the best judge of what action it is that he is performing. He knows what it is without inferring it from the behavioral events, since some behavioral events may not be undertaken and none hang together in intelligible ways until they are meaningfully related to each other by their ingredience in this specific action.

2. Spectator I does not have, usually, as good reason for his answer to the question "What was the actor doing?" as the agent does, and in any event his reasons for his answer are different from the agent's. The Actor-for-Spectator I may be very different from the agent in propria persona, and Spectator I may give a very different answer from that of the agent. Spectator I can answer "The child is doing his homework," because both he and the child know the patterns of behavior exacted of someone doing his homework, and his observations (which are optically just like those of Spectator II) show that the child's behavior comprises events that are the appropriate ones if his action is that of doing homework. He sees, in the strict optical sense, only what Spectator II sees, but instead of seeing the child "as a moving body," he sees the child "as studying," because he employs a criterion of relevance and functional equivalence of behavioral events that Spectator II does not use (or at least in his role as physiologist has no right to use).

But Spectator I can give some account of the child's action that the child cannot give (or at least that the child can give only when he takes the difficult supernumerary role of being a spectator of himself). There may be background information that Spectator I has which explains the child's action *as a whole*, that is, explains the child's action of doing his homework, just as "doing his homework" explains the sub-actions ingredient in it and the relevant behavioral events that are occurring. Spectator I may say, "The child is studious" or "The child is ambitious"; he thus classifies the child according to his traits, dispositions, or motives and explains why he does his homework every night, and not just on this one occasion. The child can be genuinely ignorant of the truth of the statement "He is studious," while yet confirming it by his habitual behavior.

The agent is in a better position to know his intention than the spectator is; he can hardly make a mistake (though he may lie) about what he intends to do, but he may subsequently look back upon his action as a spectator and revise his account of it. The child may think "doing his homework" is an adequate description of what he is doing but may later decide that though doing his homework was what he was doing, doing his homework in order to impress his parents is what he was *really* doing. The spectator is often in a better position than the agent to know this larger story, and therefore can give a better account of the agent's action than the agent himself can. He can refer to motives, traits, and habits that the agent has but does not know he has. These are all background factors that make it intelligible to the spectator that the actor has the specific intentions he has, and when the spectator inquires into the actor's motives it is usually a sign that the actor's intentional act, or rather why he has just that intention and no other, is not understood by the spectator. An actor may resent inquiry into his motives because it suggests that an action, perfectly intelligible to him, appears dissembling to another. It is almost as if motives were discreditable things had only by people under suspicion. (I would resent it if someone asked me my motive for doing some act of ordinary courtesy.)

But explanations given by spectators in terms of the actor's motives need not always leave this bad taste. Like explanations by reference to traits and habits, they explain intentional acts (and sometimes unintentional acts) by relating them to one another in a narrative that makes sense of each. Intentions shape single acts (like sharpening a pencil and adjusting the light) into complex intentional acts (such as preparing homework); motives shape complex acts (like doing homework and competing in sports) into intelligible extended segments of life history. Since most men cannot back away from rather short sequences of intentional acts so as to see their lives as wholes and the underlying continuities that connect their disparate intentions, they never discover what their deepest motives and most pervasive traits are; hence few men can write good autobiographies. A good biographer can understand the actor better, perhaps, than the agent understood himself—and this in spite of the fact that good biographers repeatedly have to confess their puzzlement about exactly what, at a particular moment, the actor's intention was.[4]

4. The distinction between motives and other reasons for actions, especially intentions, is subject to much recent inquiry that has had but

3. Spectator II is either a fool or a physiologist. He does not see the child doing his homework because there is no such behavioral event as doing homework. "Doing homework" is not a value for any variable in a physiological law, as "twitching of the eyelid" may be. The question Spectator II asks is: "Why (= because of what cause) did the events take place which my colleague Spectator I calls 'writing' but which we physiologists describe as . . ." (and here follows a long description of the behavioral events which occurred). The answer demanded is in terms of a history referring to reinforcements by conditioning, physiological states, stimuli, and covering laws. To give such an answer does not require knowledge of institutions like schools and rules of doing homework, and physiologists do not talk of ambition or studiousness in their explanations (even if they carelessly admit them into their questions). The physiologist tries to describe the state of the child's body and its history of conditioning, the stimulus that occurred, and the behavioral events just subsequent to the stimulus and to connect them together by a law that excludes any suggestion that one

few firm results. R. S. Peters, in *The Concept of Motivation* (New York, 1960), chap. 2, thinks of motives as functioning in the appraisal of aberrant behavior; Alan R. White, in *The Philosophy of Mind* (New York, 1967), pp. 136–38, argues that 'motive' signifies a *kind of explanation,* not a *kind of reason.* But Alfred Schutz, in *The Phenomenology of the Social World* (Evanston, 1967), pp. 88, 91, distinguishes between "because-motives" and "for-the-sake-of-motives," and G. E. M. Anscombe, in *Intention* (Oxford, 1957), §13, identifies "forward-looking motives" (roughly like "for-the-sake-of-motives") with intentions. I can only conclude that "motive" is ambiguous and serves many functions in the explanation of action; in the text I have tried to take account of both the Peters and the Schutz analysis.

of the events happened for the *sake* of another. The law is one which permits him simply to foretell what will happen next time if one or more of these variables is changed.[5]

This is a noble program and aspiration. Its greatest achievements have been won in the explanation of behavioral events which can be moulded into complex actions chosen by the spectator. There is no reason to think that physiology and operant conditioning cannot give us the whole story about behavioral events like muscle contractions. But in people, physiology is not the whole story, not because there is a soul or entelechy or élan vital in the presence of which the laws of physiology break down; rather it is because there is another story to which physiological knowledge is almost wholly irrelevant. (Notice that I did not say *physiology* is irrelevant, but only physiological *knowledge; physis* is relevant, but not our *knowledge of physis.*)

What makes the second spectator's account largely irrelevant to the agent's and the first spectator's is twofold: it is his vocabulary and his grammar. The second is more significant than the first.

5. Skinner, who is neither fool nor physiologist but in some other respects like Spectator II, holds that "operant behavior is the very field of purpose and intention," but says that calling a bit of behavior purposive does not explain it; rather, we call it purposive because it is behavior that has been reinforced by like contingencies in the past and is therefore the event that will most probably occur in the present contingency and is preparatory for its outcome; the future event (the end) is not effective, and Skinner rejects the effort "to find a prior representative of a future consequence" among the conditions of an intentional act. In sum, he does not acknowledge a difference between intentional and purposive behavior, and gives a reductive explanation of the latter. See *About Behaviorism*, pp. 55, 128–29 and passim.

Spectator II talks about muscles and nerves because he can see these things, though we can hardly forbid him the use of expressions like "holding the pen," which are not in the purified observational language of physiology; "holding the pen" is just a little infected with action but can be broken down into more elementary responses of which the agent could give no account because he is not conscious of them. But what does the scientific spectator do with such concepts? He puts them into a causal context so that whatever meaning they have is the meaning they have for the spectator to whom they are values in causal laws. Thus Skinner: "A person acts intentionally . . . not in the sense that he possesses an intention which he then carries out, but in the sense that his behavior has been strengthened by [past] consequences [of like behavior]." [6]

Even if we go far beyond the limits of strict physiological talk about things observable by physiologists and let Spectator II talk of ideas, sensations, intentions, emotions, and other so-called "mentalistic entities," it helps him little in talking sense about what the child is doing so long as he maintains that the proper explanation is in terms of these entities or processes related as causes to effects. Pushes and pulls are still pushes and pulls even if they be mental instead of physical; and if we are to talk scientifically about

6. *Beyond Freedom and Dignity*, p. 108. The behavior and the intention (if the intention is a "mental event") have the same causes in the previous history of the organism. Skinner's gloss upon "intention" does not, incidentally, distinguish between intentional and habitual acts, and what he says here of intention might be uncontroversial if said about habit.

pushes and pulls or causal conditions, it is far more parsimonious to talk about those the spectator can see than those with which the agent alone is acquainted. A spiritual automaton has no advantages over a mechanical automaton; it is hidden from the prying eye of the physiologist, but it is still an automaton, and an automaton is not an agent, for an automaton does not act, it reacts. For the perfect Spectator II there are no agents: "There is no place in the scientific position for a self as a true originator or initiator of action." [7] Talk of agents' doing something is a sign of our ignorance: "If we do not know why a person acts as he does, we attribute the behavior to him." [8] This means that to Spectator II, anything that Spectator I says that cannot be translated into his language is obscurantist nonsense. But Spectator II does not believe that Spectator I does in fact say anything that cannot be translated into his language and thereby gain in clarity and explanatory power.

But surely the agent thinks that what he and Spectator I are saying cannot be so translated. The agent does not know all the facts that Spectator II knows, so we might suppose that Spectator II is the better judge of what is really going on. But the agent cannot believe this without self-stultification; he could at most say, "I have been so conditioned to say 'What Spectator II says is true' that I say it." But if that is his reason for saying it, he has no reason for believing the content of the *enclosed* quotation; and if he does

7. B. F. Skinner, *About Behaviorism*, p. 225.
8. B. F. Skinner, *Beyond Freedom and Dignity*, p. 58.

genuinely believe it, he has no reason for believing the *entire* quotation.

The differences between the first two and the third answers describing what the child is doing show that descriptions are not conceptually neutral; they are structured by the questions they answer or by the way a single question is interpreted.

Seeing is more than an optical phenomenon; one sees more than stimulates his eyes; seeing is getting optical evidence to answer a specific question or carry out a specific task. It is procuring data for acts of construction which, being conducted according to tacit or explicit rules, can be performed in much the same manner and lead to much the same answer even if the optical data are different, as they always are even when two different observers are carrying out the same task. But the optical data can be very much alike and yet give rise to different descriptions when an observer shifts his task from that of answering one question to that of answering another. There are no immaculate perceptions (Nietzsche: *unbefleckte Erkenntnis*); the optical facts do not speak for themselves, and the answers we give for them, as it were in their name, are only negatively controlled by them. Data are given, but that they are clues, and what they are clues of, is determined by the observer. "Alles Faktische ist schon Theorie," says Goethe. All of this is well known since the time of Kant, and the twentieth century has been reminded of it again by both Cassirer[9] and the pragmatists.

9. The contrast I am drawing between "optical seeing" and "observing" corresponds to Cassirer's distinction between "the mode of sight,

Seeing, in the optical sense, is a biological event; looking, that is, what the spectator does, is an action. No two people can optically see exactly the same thing, but what is observed, that which is successfully looked at as "a case in point," is called fact or object. Genuine observation is replicable (in principle, at least) by others. There are social rules of observation, and different spectators by obeying different rules of observation fill different roles and see different things. One observes as a physiologist and sees muscular contractions; another observes as a commonsense commentator on the human scene and sees homework being done. Each brings a conceptual grid to bear upon different optical sights. In the case of the physiologist, this conceptual grid is one that cannot be mastered except by learning; it can be taught, articulated, corrected, and wilfully changed.

The situation of the first spectator is epistemologically like that of the second, but technically and practically vastly different. The commonsense spectator is interested in answers to questions that cannot be framed in the language of the second spectator, but he cannot optically see anything the second spectator cannot. The commonsense spectator has not learned (or at least does not remember learning) how to make commonsense observations and to give commonsense answers; he may not even be aware of what he brings

which consists of a mere receptivity to impressions of light and their differences, and the mode of vision, in which our intuitive world is built up." *Philosophy of Symbolic Forms* (New Haven, 1957), 3:124–25. See also the important argument that "symbolic ideation first constitutes vision," p. 134.

to bear upon what he optically sees, or of the fact that in interpreting what he optically sees he is following rules that have social sanctions. Being oblivious of these conceptual constraints, he may think he is seeing "things as they are" and "real people" and make invidious comparisons between the "real world" he grasps and the "partial pictures" painted from peculiar perspectives by physiologists, phrenologists, economists, and others who take "narrow" views.

In part the commonsense spectator is justified in his feelings of superiority. His world view may not be metaphysically right and theirs wrong, but his canvas is large enough to contain pictures of physiologists and pictures of their pictures; it may indeed have on it a great many simple facts of physiology known to him and not merely to physiologists. His language is a lingua franca in which spectators each with his own language can communicate with others. The commonsense world is a common world. One can understand the common world without knowing much physiology, but one cannot talk the language of physiology— or at least have anyone to talk to—unless one knows the commonsense language in which one can talk about his reasons for making specific observations and the validity of the inferences to be drawn from them.

But in another respect the commonsense spectator is not justified in his feelings of superiority. He is naive; he thinks he sees things and people as they really are. This is a foolishness that very little experience ought to remove (though it often does not). It is a foolishness to which mature people are intellectually superior, for they acknowledge, perhaps grudgingly, that their so-called "impressions" of people may be egocentric and prejudiced and subject to correction by comparison with those of others. My social world is not characterized by the same degree of objectivity and intersubjective agreement as the physiologist's world; it isn't a "world" at all, but an egocentric view of or perspective on a world whose structure and contents are to be known only by an anonymously ideal observer or angel. It is up to me to *try* to see a man "as he really is" just as it is up to the physiologist to try to see a muscle twitch "as it really does." The opinion of the individual physiologist is no more a fact about the muscle than my opinion of another man is a fact about that man, but physiologists have learned better to correct their opinions and to report facts by the explicit formulation of rules of evidence and inference than commonsense spectators have. There are institutions in our society that make physiologists talk objectively; there are none that make ordinary men, politicians, and philosophers talk objectively and say the same thing. Poincaré somewhere says that the difference between a common language and a technical scientific language is that more people understand the former; I would add, a larger fraction of the users of the latter agree on what to say in it.

In commonsense language we talk about other people's thoughts and feelings with almost the same familiarity and assurance that we talk about our own. I do not know of any philosopher before Descartes who was puzzled by this or inquired as to how it is possible and whether it is justified. Since he raised the problem, no solutions to it have enjoyed universal approbation. With a few notable exceptions, philosophers who have seen the problem have worked from the premiss that we *really* know only what we incorrigibly know, like the immediate certainty I have that some experiences (toothache being, for some strange reason, the paradigm) can be ascribed to me, and that anything else I know is derivative from this kind of certainty pieced out with hypothesis or built from it by logical construction, and therefore stands in need of justification. With such premises as these, there arises what Kant called "the scandal of philosophy" and the seeming impossibility of proving that there is an external world independent of my experience. The failure of arguments to show that some of the things in the world are animated by minds with experiences like my own is a secondary scandal. Given the usual kinds of arguments for the existence of other centers of consciousness, the easy refutations of them are of such a kind that, if thrust all the way home, they would not only leave me unjustified in my claim to know that there are other minds; they would equally well cast doubt on my claim to know that *I* have a *body*.

For reasons already mentioned, I do not wish to discuss the problems of other minds as if the threat of solipsism had to be met on a battleground chosen by the skeptic in his role of solipsist. Rather, I want to show that much of the discussion of the problem of other minds has been vitiated by use of the wrong model, as if the data of Spectator II were hard data while the data of Spectator I were soft data, or not data at all but only conjectures. It is then supposed that we must make a mysterious transition from the hard knowledge of physiology to derivative knowledge that other bodies incorporate minds. To see the actions of an actor and not just the contractions of his muscles is sometimes interpreted as if it had to result from an inferential step from the hard facts of behavior to the fuzzy area of personal understanding. This is an incorrect model, however, because neither temporally nor epistemologically are the facts of physiology prior to those of the commonsense view of another person: not temporally, for we are born into a commonsense world and not into a physiological laboratory; and not epistemologically, for the optical data that ultimately control all our judgments are not data that already fit, to a preeminent degree, the framework of physiology. It is not that we cross an epistemological or inferential bridge when we go from knowledge of bodies to knowledge of agents, from muscle contractions to actions, from physiology to psychology; we do not cross that bridge because there is no such bridge to cross.

The knowledge the first spectator has is not derived from the kind of knowledge the second has, but it is got in ways that are epistemologically similar. Because we understand how Spectator II sees and explains a muscle contraction better than we understand how Spectator I sees the child's anger, however, we may use the former as a model for interpreting the latter. The analogy does not entail the use of the physiologist's knowledge as a premiss in the justification of the knowledge claimed by the first spectator. To confuse a model in *our* interpretation of the first spectator's knowledge with a premiss for the first spectator's own knowledge is to commit what William James[10] called "the psychologist's fallacy."

What I am about to say makes no pretence to be a genetic account of how an infant's blooming, buzzing confusion gets organized into knowledge of the commonsense and physiological realms of discourse. To interpret it so would once again be to commit the psychologist's fallacy. I do not know whether infants first live in blooming, buzzing confusion or not, and whether language is the organizing factor which reduces it to order, as Cassirer taught.[11] I am concerned only to give a justificatory rather than a genetic account of two different kinds of knowledge. The question is: how can optical and other data function in knowledge of both people and muscles? How can we go from seeing the same undefined things (which I have called optical seeing) to seeing arms move because muscles contract, and to seeing an angry boy throw down his pen in frustration because he cannot solve a problem?

All three are seeings, and none has a better right to this name than the others. I can see what I cannot or do not describe or classify without applying interpretative and nonoptical categories. I can describe it by saying what I see it *as;* I can see *that* there is a muscular contraction or the expressive act of a frustrated boy. *Seeing as* and *seeing that* underlie both commonsense and physiological knowledge.

In saying "I see a living muscle" I am going beyond

10. *Principles of Psychology* (New York, 1904), 1:196.
11. *The Philosophy of Symbolic Forms* (New Haven, 1955), 1:198, 268.

what I optically see in very much the same way as
when I say "I see a frustrated boy." Neither of these
sentences uses the word "seeing" in the exclusively
optical sense; I see *something* that I take to be a living
muscle, and I see something that I take to be a
frustrated boy. The optical seeing has as its object
merely something that cannot be described in neutral
language, because there is no neutral language. Nonoptical seeing is seeing something *as* an entity of a
particular kind that can be described in languages
determined by my purposes, perspectives, and expectations. Upon the occasion of seeing something that I
take to be important, I ascribe to that something
powers that answer to my expectations of what I may
subsequently see. One optical sight is not a sign of the
next except under conditions that are not optically
sighted and cited, but which must be mentioned in the
context of raising and justifying expectations. Things
seen as things of a specific kind are of a different
logical type—whatever their metaphysical status—
from things merely optically seen.

What I have been saying is as true of seeing people
as seeing muscles. A frustrated look on the child's face
tells me that he will do some of a range of behaviorally
equivalent actions that I call "trying again" or the
like; for by the first we see him *as frustrated,* and seeing
his behavior *as the action* of trying again is confirmation
of our physiognomic seeing *that* he was frustrated.

To this extent, an analogy holds between seeing
another person as a person of a particular kind or in a
particular state of mind and in a life situation to which
that state of mind is appropriate, and seeing a flash of

light as lightning which will be followed by thunder. The analogy I wish to develop has nothing to do with the standard analogical argument by which, it has been supposed, I move from a knowledge of my own state of mind to an inference concerning that of another.[12] I am trying, rather, to point out that there is an analogy between my knowledge of another's state of mind and my knowledge of other things on the occasion of optically seeing something else. The analogy lies in the fact that both kinds of perceptual knowledge are expressed in synecdoche. It is by synecdoche that I say, "I see an iceberg," when in fact all that I optically see is the part above water.

Perception is synecdochic when I see (in one sense) the whole by seeing (in another sense) the part. Synecdochic perception is not limited to the physiognomic perception of persons and their characters by "getting an impression" of their features and gestures, but all physiognomic perception is synecdochic. Like

12. Analogy requires knowledge of three terms to permit inference to a fourth. In the standard analogical argument for the existence of another's state of mind, the three terms I would have to know are: my state of mind, my optical looks, and the actor's state of mind. But in fact I know only two terms in the analogy, namely, *my* state of mind, and *his* optical looks. I do not know how I optically look when I am angry, and until I have reason to believe that he is angry I cannot see his optical looks as angry looks. I do not deny that analogy plays a great part in our understanding of another's specific actions and states of mind; I deny only that it is an argument that another *is* acting or *has* a state of mind. The analogy is parasitic upon the synecdoche and cannot replace it. When the analogy is employed, it takes its start from a richer perceptual field than that of neutral optical seeings, and it may go in either direction; I can categorize my state of mind by seeing the resemblances between my actions and those of an actor, and on other occasions I can categorize the actor's state of mind.

any synecdochic perception, perception of agents and actions is subject to error and illusions. It is intuitive rather than consciously inferential, but it is not incorrigible. It differs from the synecdochic perception of physical objects in one important respect: what is synecdochically perceived in physiognomic perception cannot in principle be optically seen, while what is synecdochically perceived in the physical world can subsequently, at least in principle, be optically seen. I say, "I see the moon," when in fact I optically see only one hemisphere of the moon. If I became an astronaut I could optically see other parts. I cannot directly experience the excitement of the astronaut whose bodily motions I optically see on television. I could do that only by *being* him. But while it is not logically impossible for me to become an astronaut, it is logically impossible for me to become Colonel Armstrong. Hence physiognomic perception cannot be "cashed in" in such a way as to refute solipsism any more than ordinary perception (which is also synecdochic) can be used to demonstrate the continuous existence of *things* not observed. Of physical things that we believe do exist, synecdochic perception can be confirmed or disconfirmed by optical seeing; in C. I. Lewis' terminology, by confirming terminating judgments we confirm objective judgments. But the test for the synecdochic perception of another's state of mind is not some subsequent direct experience of his state of mind, for that is impossible, but more synecdochic perception of his other actions, the test lying in the coherence of the synecdoches, the dramatic unity of the episode.

To see a man as angry does not require us to see (or feel) his anger as a hidden cause known only to himself; if it did, we could never know he is angry. I may, of course, see him as angry when he does not feel angry, and as not angry when he in fact is, provided he is a gifted dissimulator. But unless there were reliable signs in behavior of what a man is inwardly feeling, we could not have synecdochic perception *even when it is wrong,* and the art of drama, where it is always wrong,[13] would be impossible.

Except in histrionic deception, anger is not a hidden state known only to the man who is angry. A snapshot of an angry man looks just like a snapshot of a man about to sneeze, but a moving picture of an angry man looks like an angry man. Anger is seen as an episode in the actor's drama, which prepares me for the next episode. I see angersome features in the world he is facing, I see angry responses by him, and I do not miss the impossible verification of *having* his feelings, which would correspond to optically seeing what was originally perceived synecdochically.

I am availing myself here of neither logical behaviorism nor the James–Lange theory of emotions, that the behavior *is* the anger and the feelings are consequent upon the behavior; that theory may or may not be true, but it is not a part of what I am saying. I am saying that in seeing behavior *as angry* I am optically seeing a part of a whole, and that I would see it differently if I believed (rightly or wrongly) that it was

13. "If Garrick really believed himself to be that monster Richard the Third, he deserved to be hanged every time he performed it." Boswell, *Life of Johnson* (New York: Modern Library, n.d.), p. 1070.

not a part of this whole containing seen angersome features and (unseen) feelings of the actor. I see his behavior as a link between angersome features and feelings and may not even notice, until a philosopher points it out, that I do not see the feelings in the same way I see the gestures, or the gestures in the same way I see his arm move. If caution makes me refrain from saying I see his anger, nothing keeps me from saying I see (and not that I infer) *that* he is angry or that I see him *as an angry man.*

When I say I am angry I am referring to, or expressing, a felt emotion of my own. But I learn the name of this felt emotion and how to report or express it in words in much the same way that I learn what is the character of the emotion another expresses. I do so by employing the same vocabulary others use in describing and assessing situations that provoke felt anger in me. I learn to communicate about my feelings in very much the same way I learn to detect from their communication what the feelings of others are and what feelings they are ascribing to me. Behavior that is provoked and observed is the angry behavior of another person; the emotion that is provoked and felt is my own. There are two wholes having a common part, namely the situation. Only because we believe that much the same things as sized up by different people call forth like responses do we have a use for the word "anger" and know how to use it in reference to ourselves and others; and if I find a situation that seems to anger another but is not at least potentially angersome for me, I may have difficulty deciding whether he is angry, or I am insensitive.

Since Hegel's time it has become a cliché that self-knowledge is very much like our knowledge of another, and that when formulated in language it is parasitic upon our language for knowledge of another. When I observe myself, the I that is observed is an actor, and that actor is as subject to being judged by the agent I am as any other actor. Robert Burns was right about how hard it is "to see oursels as ithers see us," but it is not impossible. Both my self-knowledge and knowledge of another actor are synecdochic. I feel my emotions and I do not feel another's, but I learn what they are, what they are called, how they are appropriately expressed by watching other people respond to what I believe is the same public world having the same emotion-provoking features, listening to what they say, and speaking the same language. I believe that my behavior yesterday was angry behavior not because I observed it, but because I was in an angersome situation and felt anger; I believe you were angry yesterday, because I saw your angersome situation and saw your behavior. There are two wholes, you in your mise-en-scène and I in mine; I "see" two parts of one of these wholes and two parts of the other. There is an overlap of only one of the parts I see, our more-or-less common world, but the wholes have the same structure, and by synecdoche I imaginatively supply the missing part.

But perhaps someone thinks it would be less mysterious and a contribution to clarity if we recognized that Spectator I did not "really see" the actor's anger or frustration, and that his claim to do so was just seeing one thing and thinking of something else that could not be *really* seen. Perhaps we could remove some of the mystery of our social knowledge if Spectator I were more cautious in his observational claims. Perhaps the social sciences should draw a distinction between what one *sees* and what he *infers*, as the natural sciences are supposed to have done. That would give data for our social and interpersonal knowledge as hard as those that Spectator II has in the natural sciences; and with this firm a foundation perhaps the second spectator's observations could be a model of what Spectator I's commonsense observations ought to be, and our social sciences could be built on hard data into structures as stable as those of physics and chemistry.

Very well, I would be willing to try, provided that what is offensive in the commonsense language of Spectator I is also removed from the scientific language used by Spectator II. But as long as he is permitted to say, "I saw a reinforced response" instead of what he *optically* saw, with no infection of theory, Spectator I should be allowed to say, "I saw the child grow angry." No useful language is tied down to phenomenalistic reports; commonsense language is not the only one that fails to be theoretically neutral and sterile against the spectator's assumptions. There is no more immaculate perception in physics than in sociology, and common language is not the only one that employs synecdoche.

Throughout these pages I have been using the word "actor" metaphorically, as if a man bent upon the serious business of life were an actor in a play and insulated from the workaday world. A metaphor like "All the world's a stage and men and women merely players" is a half-truth masquerading as a whole truth. But this half-truth is a pregnant one. If we know how I come to see a man, with whom I may have real-life dealings, as an actor in the literal sense of the word, we may better understand how I can see him as an actor in the metaphorical sense when he is going about in the everyday world.

Simply dressing up in a costume and performing various actions on a stage does not make a man an actor in the literal sense. He must act in ways determined by a ritual, script, or plot, in an aesthetic space insulated from the causal nexus and the space and time of real life. The props, costumes, proscenium, and audience mark out these discontinuities, and put the spectator in a frame of mind to see a person as an actor in the literal sense of the word even if the spectator does not know the script he is following. If, however, I as spectator do know the plot of *Hamlet*, I am in a better position to understand the stage action than Hamlet is (though obviously not able to do so better than Lord Olivier, whom I see *as* Hamlet), for I know some things that Hamlet does not know and am better able to interpret his motives and foresee their issue than he is. I know that Hamlet is going to die in the last act, but Hamlet does not know this, and I am enabled to see each of his actions in the light of the whole plot, to have an insight that Hamlet himself does not attain until the very end. The plot as a whole is condensed into each action, and the perception of the literal actor in an unreal world is thoroughly synecdochic, since the whole is given to me before any single part is perceived.

If, on the other hand, I do not know the plot of *Hamlet*, my mode of interpreting the actions that Lord Olivier performs as Hamlet is very much the same as my mode of interpreting the actions I observe him to perform in real life as a member of the House of Lords. The reasons, situation, and specific public conditions of practice of the stage world of Elsinore Castle are different from but no more strange to me than those of Westminster Palace, and the manner in which I understand his actions in each is the same. My perception of the *literal actor in an unreal world* is synecdochic in the same experimental, tentative way as my perception of the *metaphorical actor in the real world*.

3: REASONS, RULES,

AND CAUSES

The words *reasons* and *causes* are often used inter-
changeably. Ordinarily, "the reason it rained" is the
same as "the cause of the rain"; and "The letter from
Paris caused me to change my plans" means the same
as "The reason I changed my plans was the letter from
Paris." Socrates had heard that Anaxagoras gave a
reason for everything, and was disappointed to find
that he gave only one kind of reason, namely the
causes of the behavioral events involving his bones and
muscles in sitting in prison, and not the "true cause" of
his action, namely "that [he] thought it better and
more right to remain here and undergo [his] sentence"
(*Phaedo* 98–99). It is not quite correct to say that one is
a false cause and the other a true cause; it is a question
of *what* it is that is caused. Socrates was interested in
the "true cause" of his action in submitting to punishment, while Anaxagoras was interested in explaining
the events taking place in his body. These two accounts
refer to what happened in the same stretch of time and
part of space, but they refer to it under different
descriptions, so that his sitting there appears to be one
thing and his acquiescing in his punishment another.
Had Socrates on the day of his death stood at the door
instead of sitting on his couch, Anaxagoras would have
had to give a different explanation for a different
event, while Socrates' explanation of his action would
have been unchanged. Socrates was interested in the
cause of an action that could have been carried out in
two ways (sitting or standing), while Anaxagoras was
interested not in that action but in the sitting as an
effect of motions of bones and muscles.

While ordinary folk frequently use *cause* and *reason* as

synonyms or near synonyms, philosophers have recently preferred to use *cause* in giving explanations of changes in physical objects including behavioral events in living bodies, and to use *reasons* in the explanations of actions of persons, and this has given rise to the vigorous debate as to whether reasons really are causes. The verbal convention has roots in the Humean analysis of the concept of cause, but by itself, of course, it solves nothing; we cannot verbally legislate that reasons and causes are so different that acting from a reason is metaphysically different from being caused to behave, and we must make sure that in following the now-conventional distinction between reasons and causes we do not beg any important questions. Keeping this precaution in mind, I will say, "The cause of the metal's expanding was the heat," "Lack of oxygen caused him to faint," "A loose rug caused him to slip and break his leg," but "The reason he went into the house was the heat in the garden."

There are as many species of explanation by citing reasons for an action as there are kinds of reasons that people have for their actions. For example, all the following are explanations of the same action by different formulations of its reason: "His motive for going into the house was curiosity," "His intention was to find out who was there," "His purpose was to find out who was visiting his family," and even (though this involves an ambiguity we shall try to avoid) "The arrival of visitors caused him to stop working in his garden and return to the house." All of these give perfectly ordinary reasons, universally understood, for his returning to the house. There are subtle differences between them, but the differences and connections between them are, for these discussions, less important than finding what, if any, generic differences there are between causes and reasons as these are distinguished in post-Humean practice. Is the difference merely a difference in the kind of things to be explained, namely events and the special kind of events we have called actions?

Giving either reasons (in all its subvarieties) or causes constitutes responses to "why?" "Why?" expresses our puzzlement, and requests information or reassurance that will reduce our puzzlement or defer it for later handling when we ask "why?" about something else that was mentioned in answer to the first why question. The question "why?" is answered when the asker of the question can candidly say, "I see." The only adequate judge of the appropriateness (not the correctness) of an answer is the person who asked the question.

To ask "why" in the sense of "because of what cause?" according to the tradition demands an answer that has at least the following characteristics. It refers to an event not later in time than the event to be explained or a state simultaneous with the state to be explained. It does so with an implicit generality, in that the causal explanation of an event is likewise an explanation of all events that in relevant respects are like the specific event to be explained (but finding out what these "relevant respects" are may be a major part of discovering the cause, for the relevant respects may be hidden from the first view). It makes this implicitly general claim that the event or state mentioned in the explanation is always sufficient to bring about events or states relevantly like this one to be explained, so long as *other* states and events are the same, but this ceteris paribus clause cannot be so comprehensive and the relevancy condition so stringent that the claim to generality is trivialized. The connection between causes and effects must be strong enough to support counterfactual statements such as "If there were a current in this wire, it would heat up," yet not so strong as to be analytic, like "If I were to marry, I would have a wife." Finally, if we say that one thing or event is the cause of another it must be possible to identify whatever event or state it is that is said to be the cause independently of identifying the event or state to be explained, and independently of the knowledge that the first is in fact the cause of the second. There must be in this (or in other relevant cases) evidence of the existence or occurrence of the cause that is independent of the knowledge that the effect has occurred.

Many singular events that are explained causally in a narrative do not seem to meet all of these conditions; certainly it is not known that they do, and singular events therefore are predicted only with some probability, not certainty. But all scientific explanations that explain specific kinds of events by appeal to a causal or functional law of nature meet these conditions, and it is at least arguable that for every single event that is explained causally there is assumed to be a universal law that covers it.

Where the covering-law model of explanation seems least applicable, namely unique historical events, the events involve people with reasons. "Caesar's crossing the Rubicon caused the civil war" can be explained better in terms of reasons than of causes, when "cause" is not just a synonym for "reason" and involves the covering-law conception. The covering law might be something like this, though far more specific in its details: "Whenever a triumphant general crosses the Rubicon with his army intact, the Senate responds by making war upon him." We do not know whether this is true or not, but we do not need to know in order to say "Caesar's crossing the Rubicon caused the Senate to do such and such," for the latter is ordinarily interpreted as equivalent to "The Senate's reason for doing so and so was that Caesar had crossed the Rubicon," and the latter statement is intelligible without the assumption that the Senate would act this way in all similar cases (and it is, in fact, obvious that the Senate would not do so).

It was Kant's thesis in the Second Analogy of Experience that while the discovery of specific causes is entirely empirical, Hume was wrong in thinking that the principle of causality itself is empirical. Rather, Kant saw it as an a priori (unfalsifiable) principle or regulative rule that the observer uses in the interpretation of what he optically sees (intuits), by virtue of which the intuition of mere appearances is converted into the perception of objects and objective happenings. We need not, for our present purposes, put Kant's own phenomenalistic interpretation upon objects and happenings in order to see the importance of his theory that the proposition "Every event has a cause" has a different origin and function from those of any specific statement about what causes what. One expresses a demand the knower makes upon experience if it is to be intelligible; the other is the answer experience gives.

The principle that actions have reasons is analogous to this. Armed with the concepts of reason and cause, we dichotomize occurrences into those the explanations of which involve causes and those which are explained by reasons. Just looking at an occurrence will not tell us whether it is a complex event or an action. With the growth of knowledge we may reclassify happenings: we used to think a man's getting drunk was an action done for a reprehensible reason; now we may think it an event caused by a vitamin deficiency. We used to think of a slip of the tongue as an event, until Freud showed it was an action to be understood by knowing a reason for it.

Kant held that any occurrence that has a reason also has a cause, and therefore that human actions are predictable in the same way that eclipses are predictable; namely, by knowledge of their causes, even though he remarks that it seems to "conflict with equity" [1] to punish a man for what he was caused to do. His grounds for thinking this lie in aspects of his theory of knowledge that are not precisely relevant here. Kant is here taking the "angel's point of view," because the spectators in the situation are never in a

1. *Critique of Practical Reason*, Ak. 99. But in *Anthropology from a Pragmatic Point of View*, trans. Gregor (The Hague, 1974), §51, p. 84, Kant discusses the casuistical problems raised by "physical disorder of the soul's organs" causing "an unnatural transgression of the law of duty" where we lack (as we must "without dissection") "deep enough understanding of the mechanical element in man" to explain and foresee the action.

position to face this problem of "equity." For when the spectators know *what* are the causes of an occurrence in someone's body and do not merely accept the schematic principle that it must have some cause, the explanation in terms of reasons is revoked. This is especially evident when the *causes* of an actor's doing something can be located in an *action* of another person, such as a hypnotist who controls the actor by suggestion; it seems almost as if causal explanation of putative actions leaves the spectator with a surplus of unused blame and he looks for some proper target for it, such as the actor's ancestors or early environment.[2] Rather than a perfect coincidence of causation and action by reason, which may be true schematically and from the angel's point of view, there is for us an inverse relation between the successful explanations by Spectator I and Spectator II.

The difference between Spectator I and Spectator II lies in the way they interpret what they optically see. Objects are thought of (by both spectators) as things characterized by the power to produce effects in regular ways when affected by changes in other things, the powers discovered empirically or hypothesized and the responses to other things expressed in empirical laws of nature. Actors are thought of, by Spectator I, as beings characterized by abilities to act, where to act means not to respond in a uniform way to a stimulus

2. Cassius: Have not you love enough to bear with me/When that rash humour which my mother gave me/Makes me forgetful?

Brutus: Yes, Cassius; and from henceforth,/When you are overearnest with your Brutus,/He'll think your mother chides, and leave you so [*Julius Caesar*. IV. iii. 119–24].

described in physicalistic terms in a causal law, but to respond in variable ways depending upon the meaning of a situation to the actor who has a reason for the response he makes. Causal explanation depends upon empirically establishing a contingent but universal or probable connection between two independently recognized events. Explanation by reasons is just as empirical as explanation by causes, but the connection is not between two independently recognizable events or features of the events. "What a situation means" and "what reasons the actor had" are not independent variables, but must be jointly ascertained by interpreting the transaction as an episode in the history of the situation and the life-history of the actor.

Thus there is an analogy between Kant's theory of causation for Spectator II and a theory giving a comparable categorial analysis of the world for agents and for Spectator I. This was not seen by Kant, and it was left to Schopenhauer to point out the analogies between the various applications of the principle of sufficient reason. The principle that actions have reasons gives a transcendental rule for recognizing some happenings as actions of agents. To find out if some happening is an act, try to find the agent's reason for it; just as Kant held, to find out if some change in our perceptual field is a change in objects, try to find a causal law that fits it.

So long as the debate among Kant scholars is unsettled as to whether the Second Analogy of Experience is analytic or synthetic, it is too venturesome to insist on an analytic or on a synthetic interpretation of the principle of reasons. But there is as much ground for supposing that the principle of reasons is synthetic as to suppose the causal principle is synthetic. The concept of event does not, according to Kant, analytically contain the concept of having a cause; "uncaused event" is not like "unmarried wife." But to *pick out* something as an event requires a rule, and this rule is that it be assigned a fixed temporal relation to other events; that is, that its occurrence be determined by its relation to other occurrences according to a law. Likewise "irrational action" and "an act done for no reason" are not self-contradictory expressions (though in ordinary usage they generally refer to actions done for bad or poor reasons, not to actions done for literally *no* reason), but in order to find out whether some behavioral events constitute an action, we try to find out whether that segment of behavior had a reason or not. A twitch of the eye is not a wink unless it fits into a larger story of a flirtation.

There are some marked resemblances and equally marked dissimilarities between finding a reason and finding a cause. These resemblances and differences vary to some extent depending upon the kind of reason sought for, whether, for example, it is an intention or a motive. But rather than going through a lengthy comparison of each species of reasons as explanations, let us take an example in which the actor's wants are cited as the reason for his action. A man says, "I bought the tobacco because I wanted to." This tells us something important about the action, namely that it was voluntary and that the actor was not forced to do it, nor was it something he did absentmindedly or inadvertently. He wanted to buy it before he bought it and up to the time he bought it, and had he not wanted to buy it (ceteris paribus) he would not have bought it. Here we have an instance of a general truth, that one always does what one wants to do if one can do so and when there are no stronger reasons against doing it. In all these respects the reason explanation is like a cause explanation. But in one important respect it is very different. He (and I) could not know that he wanted to buy tobacco unless he (and I) knew what it would be like to buy tobacco; hence neither of us could identify, let alone describe, the want independently of identifying (and perhaps being able to describe) the act of buying tobacco.[3] Hence this reason explanation mentioning a want cannot be disconfirmed by empirical evidence in the way that a causal explanation could be disconfirmed. Empirical evidence could at most show that the explanation of buying tobacco for the reason that the man wanted to is inapplicable because the man really had another reason in this specific case. We might learn empirically that it is false that he bought it because he wanted to, but not that

3. Since lightning is empirically discovered to be the cause of thunder, I can and must be able to identify lightning without knowing what thunder is. Of course, once I have made this empirical discovery I can use the causal law as a *ratio cognoscendi* of lightning; I can say, "Wait a moment before you call that flash lightning; if it is, we shall hear thunder." Similarly, I am keeping to straight causal talk when I say, "Typhoid fever is caused by the typhoid germ," for what we now call the typhoid germ had to be recognizable through the microscope before it was known that it caused typhoid fever. When we discover the virus for cancer we will undoubtedly call it "the cancer virus," which we would not do if we did not know what cancer is; but it must be identifiable by *other* characteristics than the fact that it stands in a causal relation to cancer.

wanting to is not *a* reason for doing so. If a man who is thought to want tobacco does not buy it when he is in a tobacconist's shop, has the money, does not suffer a momentary fit of absentmindedness, and so forth, we do not have evidence against wanting being a reason, but only evidence that he did *not* want to buy tobacco.

We might disconfirm the judgment that *the man's reason* for buying the tobacco was that he wanted to, but not that wanting to buy tobacco is *a reason* for doing so. But when it is a question of cause, we can disconfirm both the judgment "This tobacco is dry because it was grown in Egypt," (by showing that it was grown in Turkey) *and* the law "The cause of moisture in tobacco is the moist climate in which it was grown." Refutations of reason explanations are one-step refutations; refutations of cause explanations may have these two steps. This brings out the most important difference between reasons and causes. So far as we can tell a priori, *anything* might cause *anything;* we do not find the relation of *appropriateness* or *fittingness* between cause and effect that we find between wanting to do something and doing it, and between any reason for doing something and doing precisely that. It may be debated whether wanting to do something is analytically related to doing it in such a way that it is self-contradictory to say one wants to do it but does not do it when one can and when countervailing causes and reasons are absent, but certainly it raises a legitimate question whether the want was there when the action is not done, and it does not in the least raise the question whether wanting is a reason. Hume is right in saying that upon the first experience of cold one could not know that water would freeze; but he is surely wrong in thinking that the connections between reasons and actions can be learned only by experience in the same way when he says he can see "no contradiction in supposing a desire of producing misery annex'd to love, and happiness to hatred." [4] I think I can see, if not a contradiction, at least an oddity that is absent in the denial of any specific causal connection, for though the feeling I have would not be called "love" if it were annexed to a desire to produce misery, any feeling annexed to desire to produce misery would not be *this* feeling, which naturally prompts me to do actions aimed at the happiness of the person for whom I have it. It does not just happen, I think, that *this* feeling should be annexed to *this* desire and not another.

A second example reveals even more about causes and reasons. The spectator says, "Wanting to smoke his pipe was the actor's reason for lighting it." The actor's intention in striking a match was to light his pipe, and he lights his pipe with the intention of smoking it. The actor must know the causal truth that lighting a pipe is a precondition of smoking it, but that knowledge is no reason for lighting the pipe unless he wants to smoke it. Wanting to light the pipe is not the reason for lighting it; wanting to smoke is the reason. Though the actor must know what is a causal condition of smoking in order to bring it about that he smoke, the causal precondition of smoking is not wanting to smoke but lighting the pipe. Anyone would

4. *Treatise of Human Nature*, ed. Selby Bigge (Oxford, 1888), p. 368. See the discussion of Hume and Skinner at the end of this chapter, p. 107.

have to light a pipe *in order to* smoke, but only the person who wants to smoke has a reason for lighting his pipe, and he does so for the sake of smoking.

This example shows how knowledge of causal laws can be among the reasons for acting, even though "causal law L is a reason for doing y" does not mean "L (or his believing L) causes him to do y." Causal laws are not causes of actions; but causal laws, not causes, may be reasons for actions.

To say that an action is done because of a reason is more like saying that a planet moves in an ellipse because of Kepler's laws than to say it moves in an ellipse because of a cause, Kepler's *anima motrix*. Wants, desires, inclinations, motives, drives, aspirations, traits, threats, promises, and beliefs about means to ends are the kinds of happenings, dispositions, feelings, mental events or states, and situational features that must be mentioned when giving reasons for actions, just as lightning and forces are the kinds of things that must be mentioned in stating the causes of thunder and the motion of planets. Saying that the former are reasons means that they function in reason explanations, not in causal explanations. Saying "he did so for a reason" means: there is something (a desire, wish, drive, belief, or whatnot) that if imputed by the spectator to the actor makes the action intelligible and meaningful to the spectator, and if he has given the *right* reason it is the one the actor would candidly give in his own account of the action and adhere to in any subsequent reassessment. Saying "this event had a cause," similarly, means there is something that, given a law of nature, makes the event intelligible to the spectator as a part of the order of nature. The intelligibility of each is under its own categorial condition, one a rule of reason and the other a law of causation.

The concept of reason cannot, I fear, be analyzed with the exactitude possible in the analysis of Humean causes. But at least the following seems true. *A reason for an action* is whatever makes it intelligible to Spectator I, or to spectators who are like him but may be more sophisticated (such as a psychoanalyst). *The reason for his action* is whatever consideration induced, inclined, weighed with, or decided the agent to do the action (his *practical* reason), or the consideration that he candidly avows retrospectively as having decided him to do the action, in the event that further examination leads him to reassess his action. An action may be attributed to as many reasons as there are accounts of the action in which it makes sense; some, but not usually all, may constitute *the* reason (the *real* reason), which is the one reason or set of reasons that is finally given when the spectator and the actor settle for one account of his actions rather than another. The actor, in undertaking the action, does so for a *practical* reason, but the *assessed* reason imputed to him by himself when he subsequently takes up the attitude of a spectator of his own past may be different from it: what he says he does out of righteous indignation he may later see to have been done out of resentment.

The agent's practical reason for his action has a prima facie claim to be credited. Unlike an assessed reason, it is not a hypothetical construction made up to account for actions already done. Were his practical reasons different, either he would do another action, or he would give the action he does another name. But upon retrospective assessment he may see through his practical reasons as rationalizations, and without lying change his story so that it makes better sense to him now than it did when he performed it. Such self-knowledge is the basis for remorse; the search for such self-knowledge may end in deeper self-deception or self-disillusionment, and it will be difficult to say which it is.

The process of giving and revising accounts of action is easier to observe when it is another spectator who tries to account for the actions of an agent. Here only assessed reasons are in question, since the spectator does not participate in the decision but only observes and tries to understand it. Even when the reasons appealed to by the spectator happen to be the same as the ones given by the actor, they do not function in the same way. For the actor, the assessed reasons are grounds for further practical reasons, but for the spectator they are grounds for prediction. Roy Pascal has well pointed out this division; the agent, he says,

> exists for himself as something uncompleted, something full of potentiality, always overflowing the actuality, and it is this indeterminateness and unlimitedness that he communicates to us as an essential quality of being. The biographer, on the other hand, works back, inwards, from the defined personality, the portrait, as it were; realised behaviour is for him decisive, not the conscious-ness of potentiality. The personality that strikes

the outer world as most defined must itself be conscious of multiple undertainties and unrealised possibilities.[5]

The spectator sees the sense, meaning, or purpose of the action, which is adumbrated in the synecdochic perception he has of the action as an episode in a larger story that includes bits and pieces of the actor's history, his situation, and idiosyncratic orientation, perhaps under an ideal type (as Weber denotes the explanatory model). The first mark of success is that the observed action makes sense to the spectator. Aristotle said plot was more important than character; but Heraclitus said, equally truly, that a man's character is his fate (determines his plot). The spectator in assessing reasons wants to know what is going to happen next, but to know that he must find out what kind of agent he is observing.

The stepping back from practical to assessed reasons may not lead the actor and the spectator to the same goal. The agent may delude himself, the actor may delude the spectator, or the spectator may choose the wrong ideal type and so construct a plot that fits neither the past acts nor those yet to come. As long as there is disagreement about assessed reasons, there is ground (for the angel) to believe that neither story is correct. If the first mark of success is the spectator's making sense of the agent's act and his successful prediction of subsequent acts, the second and finally decisive mark is the agent's own ratification of the spectator's account. Until the agent can candidly say,

5. *Design and Truth in Autobiography* (London, 1960), p. 18.

"Yes, that is why I did it; I now see that, but I did not before," the spectator's account is to be taken only with reservation. Though when challenged the spectator may defend his account by saying that the assessed reason he imputes to the actor is "resisted" by him and that such resistance is a corollary of the reason he has ascribed to the actor and was, in fact, expected as another episode in his story about the actor, another spectator (or the angel) may see this merely as an ad hoc hypothesis designed to insulate the spectator's account from refutation by the actor. In this impasse the technique of psychoanalysis is revealing: until the patient accepts the analyst's diagnosis, or, better, comes to it on his own, the therapy is incomplete. But I would add: the diagnosis is unconfirmed. Causes can work even if they are not known to the actor, but the test for whether a reason has been properly assessed is the actor's interpretation or reinterpretation of his act and the consequences this has for his ongoing practical reasons for still other acts.[6]

6. I have discussed the bearing of this test upon the reasons–causes distinction in "Conscious and Unconscious Motives," *Mind* 75 (1966): 155–79. The topic is important since ascription of unconscious motives, like that of causes, is exculpatory, and this has led to confusing unconscious motives with causes. An assigned reason of which the agent is unconscious does function as if it were a cause, since there is no appropriateness of the reason to the action that is recognized by the agent and leads him to do just this action. But that some forgotten event is selected by the *spectator* as the reason for the action depends upon *his* seeing the appropriateness between that event and the action he is trying to explain. Freud originally thought that psychoanalysis was an empirical science of causes, unknown to the patients, of the patients' symptoms; but when he began to doubt the veracity of the patients' recollections of sexual assaults in infancy, this causal, inductive explanation had to be

The assessed reasons ascribed to the actor are parasitic upon the practical reasons of the spectator; they are histrionically practical,[7] practical only in a thought-experiment in which the spectator, for the sake of assessing the actor, takes the role of the actor.

In trying to understand another's action—especially in obscure cases—the spectator must try out his account of the actor's action by putting himself in his shoes and immersing himself in his world and seeing if the action he did is the one the spectator would intelligibly do; he tries to see if the reasons he has hypothesized would be practical reasons for himself in this histrionic role. The features of the spectator's orientation and situation assumed in this histrionic role of the other, which would make his (histrionic) actions self-explanatory to him (in propria persona), he rightly or wrongly calls the reasons for the action the actor did. They are the reasons for the action that the spectator would have had were he the actor, and the intelligibility to the spectator of his own histrionic actions under these reasons is the archetype of the intelligibility that the spectator ascribes to the actions which the actor in fact performed.

Failure to understand another's action is to fail in this impersonation of him. The spectator may fail in

given up. The relation of unconscious wishes (or other reasons) to actions, as hypothesized by the spectator, is no more causal than the relation of conscious reasons to actions, which is recognized by both agent and spectator.

7. They can be directly practical for the spectator in another action, namely, his explaining the actor's action; laws of nature as well as other people's reasons can be practical reasons for the spectator in *his* action of observing and explaining their behavior.

this because he does not know or cannot imagine what is going on in the actor's private theatre with its own scenery and props. To understand another person, the spectator must commit the pathetic fallacy in the same way the actor does.

There is an implicit generality in reason-giving, somewhat like that of causes; reasons must hold good as reasons when seen by another.[8] Given a complete account of a person's attitudes and a complete picture of the world as it appears to him (an admittedly unattainable knowledge), the reasons given for his actions are reasons that could be as truly given for anyone just like him in a world just like his. A reason that cannot be made intelligible to others is *no* reason, not even a bad reason. To be sure, we cannot test this ideal of the generality of reasons statistically. But it suffices to note that given reasons are not credited by the spectator if they are not reasons that would suffice for him as he tries to put himself into the actor's world; if the spectator nevertheless does credit them, he thereby confesses to failure in his attempted impersonation and understanding. Reasons are not intrinsically private and unique to the man who has them in the way that feelings or drives, which may in fact *be* his reasons, can be peculiar to him. A man may do something for a reason that only he has, but its being a

8. To "hold good as reasons" does not mean "to hold as good reasons." For instance, if the child says he wrote "capitol" because he thought "capitol" was not only a noun but also an adjective, that is a reason I can credit even though it is a bad reason for writing "Washington is the capitol." But if the child were to say, "I wrote 'capitol' because I liked the smell," I would say that that did not "hold good as a reason" because it is unintelligible to me how it could be even a bad reason.

reason must be intelligible to others who succeed in their impersonation. When it is not, either the actor has failed to be rational or the spectator has failed to understand his rationality.

The reasons that a spectator imputes to the actor may be public or private, objective or subjective; they fall on a spectrum from a common world where reasons are the same for all, through the actor's unique life-world or through the specific public conditions of practice, to the inner dynamics of the actor's own personality. They come in families, not alone, though usually it suffices to mention one and the rest will come tagging along, obvious to others whose worlds and personal orientations are somewhat like those of the actor. One asks of a man: Why does he carry an umbrella? The situation reason is that it is going to rain, but there could also be an answer in terms of the man's subjective or motivational reason, namely that he does not want to get wet. Each of these answers suggests the other, and it would be stupid to ask for another reason for his carrying an umbrella when we have just been told that it is about to rain. It is only when there is dissonance between the action and the objective situation that either one of these answers is seen to be elliptical; only when a man carries an umbrella on a fine day, or does not carry one when the weather is threatening, do we want an answer to the question about *him* when we already have the answer to the question about the situation. An idiosyncratic reason is one that cannot be discerned from the situation as seen by the spectator, and to understand an idiosyncratic action requires the spectator to see the

actor's world as different from his own so as to
reestablish a normal relation of appropriateness of act
to situation precisely where the act appears inappropriate in the world presumptively shared by spectator
and actor.

Another locus of reasons lies between the idiosyncratic or normal subjective reasons and the situation
reasons. I referred to these reasons as the "specific
public conditions of practice." The objective world is
shot through with interpretations; the situation in
which an actor behaves is his *Lebenswelt*, the world as
he interprets it, but it is not a creation out of nothing.
There is a world of reasons that are created out of
nothing, however, comprising norms and rules of
practice, whether the practice be that of organizing the
impressions we have of the objective world, or of
bringing order into our life of feeling, willing, and
thinking, or of acting in ways that make ourselves
intelligible to others. There are rules of practice, of the
right and wrong ways of doing whatever it is that we
have reasons to do. Why does that perfectly normal
gentleman, utterly conventional in most of his actions,
carry an umbrella every day regardless of the weather?
Because he is an Englishman habitually conforming to
the conventions of his social class; it would be silly to
add the situation answer that he is doing it because
English weather is variable, or the idiosyncratic one
that he is fearful of giving offense. Why does an
educated speaker nicely distinguish between "I" and
"me"? Citing the rules of English grammar suffices; we
do not have to add that he wants to appear proper, or
that he is speaking to educated people who would

condemn him for a solecism. Why does the composer write *that* chord? To modulate into a new key; only if his audience, which provides the situation reason, had been more sophisticated, or had he had a different purpose (an idiosyncratic reason) would citing the rules of the diatonic scale fail to make his action intelligible. It is when rules of the specific public conditions of practice are broken that we look to some uncommon situational or subjective reason to make the action intelligible. Where actions become stylized, there is usually no need to make conjectures about the situation or the inner life of the actor to see his behavior as an instance of action of a certain kind, and no question of "interpretation" need arise. Words spoken in anger take on an "angry sound." This can be so imitated and become histrionic (in a pejorative sense) in order to hide the fact that there is no, or a different, emotion. "When love begins to sicken and decay," says Brutus of Cassius, "it useth an enforcèd ceremony" (IV.ii). Language, art, mathematics, morality, decorum, and the law are vast reservoirs of humanly created reasons, the merest allusion to which may suffice to explain actions, not all of which are done "in good faith," but all of which are "the expected things." (It was in the exploration of this realm of reasons that Cassirer made his most stunning discoveries.)

If I cannot build some story around some behavior which I observe, making it an episode in a plot, I fail to detect the point of what the actor is doing, or I decide that what he is doing has *no* point and conclude that the true explanation of the putative "action" is to be found in causes, not reasons. That is why, for instance, we look for causes of stupid mistakes ("no one in his right mind would do *that*!") or behavior so aberrant that we despair of finding reasons for it. But the actor may be enacting one story while I am responding to another; to understand him and his actions, I must learn about a new set of reasons, learn a new code for interpreting behavior, learn a new role I could take. When I understand, I will have the *aha*!-experience in seeing that he is doing just what I would do had I his reasons.

We want others to understand us too, sometimes not too well, and sometimes so much that we are willing to pay for that understanding. I do something that shocks and surprises me; I do not know the reasons for it, or at least suspect that the reasons I acknowledge are not good reasons, not reasons that will stand up under retrospective assessment, not reasons that would weigh with another rational man. Then I ask someone to tell me my reasons or help me discover them so that I can come to terms with my action or find better reasons for acting otherwise. A wiser man than I, impersonating a slightly different me, may show me my folly and save me from it.

Trollope, I think it was,[9] found himself troubled by

9. I cannot find this story in Trollope's *Autobiography*, but it can hardly be that I merely imagined it. The thought is given its highest potentiation in Pirandello's *Six Characters in Search of an Author*, when one character (The Father), who was never allowed on the stage by his author and who since his creation has lived a kind of dim half-life, says, "When a character is born, he acquires at once such an independence, even of his own author, that he can be imagined by everybody even in many other

one of his characters who repeatedly failed to show up on time in scenes planned for him. Suddenly it dawned on Trollope that this character, during the time he was "offstage," was drinking. From then on, his actions onstage made sense to Trollope, and the novel went on, though not as planned. I believe our self-knowledge is a little like Trollope's knowledge of this character he had created. We do not always know the reason for our actions until someone helps us find it. Then we understand ourselves better and can anticipate and prepare for later episodes in a plot we did not know before, for the plot we have been foreseeing was one based on a false assessment of our own character and reasons.

I have said that reasons are not causes of actions and that when the same thing (the arrival of visitors) can equally well be called the cause and the reason for the action, the word "cause" is being used in a sense very different from the one it has in science and, since Hume, in philosophy. We do not look for things already called "causes," but we look for things and events that have other names and see if they are instances in a law of nature. Nor do we look for things already called "reasons" but for other things (wants, wishes, motives, beliefs, etc.) and see if they stand in relation to the action in ways analogous to, but not identical with, the relation of a cause to its effect. The idea of cause is a criterion or a rule for the search for

---

situations where the author never dreamed of placing him; and so he acquires for himself a meaning which the author never thought of giving him" (act III).

whatever can be called a cause. The concept of a reason is a criterion or a rule for the selection of whatever can be called a reason for the action we wish to understand.

Every concept is a rule of recognition of something that is to be called by the name of the concept. A thing is that the concept of which is a rule for the selection of data which indicate its existence. The concept of a cat is a rule that authorizes me to say "that is a cat" when I hear something purry and feel something furry; "that" refers to the cat, which is purry and furry, but it does not refer to what is optically seen, namely an instance of the property purriness and furriness. Similarly, the concept of cause functions as a rule for picking out those events which satisfy the formal properties of causes, and the concept of a reason functions as a rule for picking out those states of mind, practices, or features of the life-world which, when adduced, will permit me to say I understand an observed action.

Rules are general, just as the concepts they correspond to are general; a command to shut the door is not a rule if it applies just to the one occasion on which it is delivered. A rule can be broken or followed. Action can be done in conformity with a rule, and if it is, it may also be done in obedience to the rule; I can act in conformity to a rule I do not know, but obey only a rule I do know and can break. Rules can be appropriate or inappropriate, legitimate or illegitimate, but not true or false. Rules are not things, like sensations, feelings, or causes. They are universals in that they can be known in exactly the same way by many people even though one applies them to some things and the others to other things. Rules can be openly formulated and communicated in a way that things (even feelings and diseases) cannot. It is by following the same rules and knowing that we are doing so that we can communicate with each other about what are *not* rules.

Leah Jacobs Stern[10] has formulated a useful distinction between regulative and counting rules. A regulative rule is one that can be conformed to or obeyed in action, as for example the rule that one must always move the knight to a square of opposite color. The condition under which the definition of knight is a regulative rule is that one does something for which it is a condition, namely, plays chess. A counting rule is one that can be followed or obeyed in one kind of action only, namely, in specifying what is to count as (for instance) a legal move in chess. Regulative rules are rules for agents, and counting rules are rules for spectators.

Causal laws of nature are not rules which the planets obey; if a planet does not appear at a predicted point, it is not breaking Kepler's law but refuting it. Though causes are not rules, causal laws may be rules, but not regulative rules for the things that instantiate them by conforming to them. Kepler's laws can be obeyed as counting rules by astronomers in their decision whether to call something a planet or not, and

10. Leah Jacobs Stern, "Empirical Concepts as Rules in the Critique of Pure Reason," *Akten des IV. Internationalen Kant-Kongresses* 2 (1974): 158–65, following a suggestion by G. C. J. Midgley, *Proceedings of the Aristotelian Society* 59 (1959): 271–90.

in astronomers' predicting positions they serve as regulative rules.

Causal laws, not causes, may thus be reasons and rules for actions of spectators. Causal laws function also as regulative rules for the guidance of agents whose actions are not just observings and explainings. Kant says that everything in nature, including man, "works according to laws" but only a rational being "has the capacity of acting according to the conception of laws."[11] Knowing the causal law "no fire, no smoke" is knowing a rule obedience to which is a condition of the intentional action of lighting one's pipe. Only by knowing this law and using it as a rule can anyone do the action; only by knowing that the actor uses this law as a rule is the spectator able to understand the action and count striking the match as an intentional act. If the agent believes a law of nature that is not recognized by the spectator, the spectator either will not understand the action or will try to imagine what the world looks like to the actor (find what the actor believes the causal law is) in such a way as to make the action intelligible to him. He learns to substitute the actor's world for his own as the stage on which the action occurs. It is thus, for example, that Cassirer was enabled to understand acts of magic. What the agent believes to be true about the world is normative for his action; but if the spectator's world-view is different, the putative truths about the actor's world are not normative and rightly so in his estimation. They explain the action that was governed by them, but they do not

11. *Foundations of the Metaphysics of Morals*, Ak. 412.

govern any actions of the spectator other than his explaining, unless (as may happen) he gives up his view of the situation and accepts the actor's view and the actor's rules.

The model of rule-following where the rules correspond to putative or real laws of nature or the conventions of practice (including the rules of language) is very useful in understanding intentional behavior, when what is intended is based upon the agent's and the spectator's having, or reaching, a common assessment of the situation in its objective and causal features. Even if I know little of the actor and his situation, most of his practices are intelligible to me if we both know the rules of language, decorum, and the legal system. If I know what a man wants, I have pretty good rules for predicting how he will act, especially if he and I size up the situation in the same way. But the model is not so directly applicable to the understanding of expressive behavior where we look for idiosyncratic reasons, look more to the wants than to the situation, since what one wants is less dependent upon observable situations than his intentions are. In an explanation by motives, we focus attention on the actor and ask, "Is he ambitious, or benevolent, or resentful?" and it is less obvious that there are rules for the expression (or the hiding) of such motives than that there are social rules that guide the intentions of a man, whether benevolent or not, who gives presents to another person. It sounds paradoxical to say that a benevolent man is following a rule when, out of genuine benevolence, he gives a present. Some of the coldness and artificiality often discerned in Kant's accounts of action depend perhaps upon the emphasis he put upon principles and rules. Yet we do say "A generous man, *as a rule*, gives presents." Here is a counting rule that the spectator can use to decide whether a man is generous or not. But how about the agent? Is there any sense in saying he is obeying a rule in showing the warmth of his feeling by giving presents? Probably not; but rules can be followed without being obeyed, and even this rule can be obeyed by a genuinely benevolent man who gives presents even when his feelings are not heated up and overflowing.

What I observe other people doing is expressible but not necessarily expressed in psychological and sociological generalizations that apply also to myself. They are norms for how I must order my life if my actions are to be intelligible to others; indeed, without this normalization of expression my inner feelings and desires may not be intelligible even to myself, or effective in my action. Mute Miltons are bound to remain inglorious and do not even have the satisfaction of enjoying their own genius. Proust wrote: "It is only with the passions of others that we are ever really familiar, and what we come to find out about our own can be no more than what other people have shewn us."[12]

La Rochefoucauld said that men would not fall in love unless they had first heard that someone else had done so (Maxim 136). Falling in love is not just having a hot, ineffable feeling. A feeling of being in love is one that is counted the right and proper feeling to be easily

12. *Swann's Way* (New York, 1970), p. 99.

expressed in actions appropriate to certain life situations as seen by the lover, but by no one else. Being in
love is the only socially acceptable neurosis; it alone
produces tolerable imprudences, delusions, and com-
pulsions. The feeling is the one that is meet, fitting,
and proper to express in deep sighs and lyric poetry.
Love is spontaneously expressed in actions that come
easy and have come to be symptomatic ones when
anyone passes for being in love, on the stage or in real
life. Tom Sawyer telling Becky what is expected of her
when she doesn't know what it means to be "engaged"
and a young gentleman looking up "the language of
flowers" in a book of etiquette are not just concerned
with decorum but are stylizing behavior so that it may
not be misunderstood; maybe also they incidentally
find out whether they themselves are "really" in love
by testing out the appropriateness of the standardized
routines to the inward feelings, which are supposed to
support them. The easy ways of expressing love serve
as counting rules for the spectator and for the loved
one, and also for the agent who, as spectator of himself,
wants to understand what is going on inside him. They
will vary from society to society and class to class, but
within each there is no wide variation, since too
unusual, idiosyncratic, and unconventional actions will
not be seen as acts in the ritual of courtship by the
beloved or assessed as expressions of love even by the
lover. One learns to fall in love in very much the same
way one learns to cook a good meal, not by preciously
introspecting on one's taste and then studying sex or
chemistry, but by learning to take a role in which one
imitates exemplary instances of the social rules that

relate desire, action, and the personal assessment of a
situation in a publicly ratified manner. If one likes the
role, he properly counts himself in love, or a good cook.
La Rochefoucauld again: "Love, however agreeable,
pleases more by the way it shows itself than by itself"
(Maxim 501).

For every action that can be performed correctly or
incorrectly, there must be a rule. For a spectator to
interpret an action there must be a rule, conformity to
which determines a justified (even if not correct)
interpretation, but neither the actor not the spectator
need know the rule in the sense of being able to
formulate it. Just as I can see depth without obeying
the laws of optics as rules, so also I can see that a man
is in love without either his or my obeying rules based
upon psychological generalizations. But we will call it
love only if we know that what he is doing passes for an
expression of love in myself and other men in our
society whom I believe to be like him. Then I can see
his action as an expression of love just as readily as I
see a hazy object as an object at a distance. A lovable
person in the situation as I see it may help me perceive
his actions as expressions of love, but if the world as I
see it is very different from the world as he sees it, such
cues may mislead me into seeing as an expression of
love what for him is only an expression of politeness. I
learn to see the world through his eyes by seeing his
actions through my own, and I learn to understand his
actions by seeing how they link him to his world as I
reproduce it in my own imagination. I do so successfully when my counting rules are the same as his
regulative rules, when the reasons I assess are his

practical reasons, and the reasons I find for his actions are the same as those he would avow.

In the order of being, I think there can be no question as to which is the more basic kind of being: minds or bodies. There are bodies without minds; so far as we know there are no minds without bodies. If one is to be explained as an effect or as a property of the other or as an emergent from the other, I can make no case for saying that in the order of being minds are the more fundamental.

In the order of knowledge, however, there is no physiology until minds and agents exist, and the establishment of a science of physiology is a recent event in the history of minds. How does it come about that a man who began his mature life as Spectator I and acts most of the time like Spectator I occupies the position of Spectator II with his view of the actor? How does this shift in perspective from seeking reasons to seeking causes occur? I shall attempt to answer this question not historically or biographically, but rather by a thought-experiment.

Suppose someone asks the question "How does a person see a distant object as having approximately the same size as he sees it to have when it is close to his eyes?" The spectator sets up an experiment that immediately polarizes a social situation and introduces an asymmetry between himself and the actor, whom he calls the subject of his experiment. Instead of seeing the situation in the same way, he makes it different. He arranges the experiment in such a way as to keep from the actor some knowledge he himself has; if he does not do this, he cannot control the experiment. He puts the actor in a dark room with discs of different sizes at different distances from the eyes, he puts a patch over one of the actor's eyes, and then he successively illuminates the different discs. Knowing the laws of optics he computes the sizes of the retinal image cast by the various objects. He asks the actor how big the various discs are. The experiment is so well known I will not take your time to describe it in any further detail; we already have enough information to illustrate the general principles in which I am interested.

The spectator discovers that the apparent size of an object (as reported by the actor) is a function of the actual size of the retinal image (as known to the spectator and unknown to the actor). He discounts the report of the actor on the sizes of the physical objects but trusts his own. He assumes the actor will answer honestly, though incorrectly, when he asks him questions; what the actor optically sees is normative for the actor's answers, but not *normative and rightly so*—that is, the spectator is under no constraint to agree with the actor about the size of the objects. He discounts the actor's reports by giving a causal explanation of the actor's behavior: stimulus and response are related as cause and effect. The actor's answer has no probative value for the spectator, for he already knows the size of the retinal image and the discs.

The spectator operates in a *context of explanation*, and the actor in an *explained context*. The explained context is always embedded in a context of explanation, and the spectator who operates in the context of explanation has at his disposal more knowledge and control over more variables than the man in the explained context.

No one is a born subject or a born experimenter; these social roles are voluntarily assumed, and—as in an introductory course in experimental psychology— each man can play each of the roles. Even a dog can be the spectator; one is reported to have said, "I've got Professor Pavlov thoroughly conditioned; every time I salivate he gives me food."

Suppose that there ensues a dispute between the student who is subject and the one who is spectator about who is right in an experiment. The subject says incredulously, "But those discs *are* the same size; I know; I saw them!" By turning on the lights and making measurements together, the asymmetry of the experimental situation and the prerogatives of the spectator are abolished and both the subject and observer, now on an equal footing, can agree. Suppose even then they do not. They appeal to a third person, who regards both the original actor and spectator as his subjects, as actors for him. He (perhaps the teacher with his superior knowledge of the mistakes students make in experiments) may discount both their reports, give a judgment that is normative and rightly so for both his actors, and try to find the causes of their divergent judgments.

It is all very well to say all action consists of behavioral events and that all behavioral events are causally related to each other; that may or may not be true—only the angel knows. But it is a very different thing to say *what* the causes of behavioral events are, for in order to do that we must so control the behavioral events that they no longer function as ingredients in the normal action of really determining the size of an object.[13] The action is defeated by the causal insult in the behavior that determines the cause, just as a Gestalt is destroyed by taking it apart and investigating each line and angle separately.

The spectator, in order to explain causally the actor's behavior, reduced the number of variables by operationally isolating some of the actor's repertoire of potential behaviors from their normal complements and prevented them from having behavioral equivalents; he reduced the normal redundancies of behaviors. Unless he does this, he cannot discover any one-to-one causal connections. In the experiment we have described, for estimating the size of the object the actor had no cue to which he could react except retinal size; in the ordinary act of looking, however, retinal size is only one of a large number of cues which would correct the judgment based on any one alone. These diverse cues are behaviorally equivalent for the ordinary actor, and this means that they are normatively equivalent—one is as good evidence as another. Different pairs of them exercise the same function in the guidance of his action; but each member of each pair

13. To be sure, the subject's asserting that the two spheres are the same size is an action; it can be made in writing or in speech, in English or in German, honestly or dishonestly, and so forth. The experimenter has not succeeded in eliminating *all* action, but the action remaining (the actor makes a verbal report) is not the one he is trying to explain; it is like a symptom of what he is seeking to explain. But the optical seeing (which is what we are trying to get at) is not an action even in the sense of "looking at" something, where our scanning a view is exploratory and guided by intelligence and purpose.

has a different cause and a different effect. To discover what these specific causes and effects are, the normal modes of the actor's actions must be suspended, and his repertoire must be restricted to that of an interesting mechanism.

Instead of a Heraclitean flux of consciousness, or a blooming, buzzing confusion, or a shifting mosaic of momentary nervous responses, each of which can be assigned a cause by the observer who has intervened to prevent normal action, there are behavioral and cue equivalences that appear to the actor as regulative, normative, and object-controlled. If they hold their own and continue to be normative for behavior in a larger context of explanation, they are normative and rightly so. Our stimuli are not causes held constant and our responses are not automatic effects, except under controlled conditions which prevent normal action. In the context of action, from their behavioral equivalences the actor constructs universals that refer not to momentary data and responses but to objects qualified by diverse data and got at along different routes. In the behavioral identification of various data as evidence of a single constant object, there is consciousness of identity of meaning and with it the possibility of substituting one pair of data for another without affecting the outcome of the action. The identity of meanings in their equifinality can function as a norm of conscious behavior only where the actual contents of consciousness lose some of their existential *hic et nunc* saliency and are seen as having the same meaning, being instances of universals that might be instantiated by other causally diverse inputs to produce the same output. Awareness of a constant object is awareness of a universal, a norm for the meaning of particular data each with its unique and unrepeatable cause. Only when an organism has developed and integrated alternative cue routes from the same situation and alternative response routes leading to the same adjustment can consciousness of objects arise. When it arises, rules of combination and substitution of symbolized meanings become available to the agent in the intelligent control of his actions. *Not memory, but goal-seeking, is the first stand of the universal in experience;* and goal-seeking by alternative behavioral routes is the first mark of agency. Only agents can know universals and can guide their behavior with respect to them; the actor is prevented by the physiologist from doing so. All the Actor-for-Spectator II can do is twitch, illustrating the laws of physiology, which are rules for intelligent actions by physiologists in explaining the behavior of the actor.

Hume and Skinner on Emotion and Action

The quotation from Hume's *Treatise*, p. 368, is conformable to the atomistic and associationistic program Hume always tries to carry out under the principle that "All beings in the universe, consider'd in themselves, appear entirely loose and independent of each other" (p. 466). Yet he admits that "love and hatred are not compleat in themselves, nor rest in that emotion which they produce, but carry the mind to something farther. Love is always follow'd by the desire of the happiness of the person belov'd, and an aversion to his misery" (p. 367). Still, he denies that "love is nothing but the desire of happiness to another person," and asserts rather that "these desires are not the same with love and hatred, nor make any essential part of them" (p. 368). He contrasts the association of ideas "which are endow'd with a kind of impenetrability, and are capable of forming a compound by their conjunction" with that of "impressions and passions [which] are susceptible of an entire union," like colors that "may be blended so perfectly together, that each of them may lose itself and contribute only to vary that uniform impression, which arises from the whole" (p. 366).

Hume is here struggling with two of his most intractable problems, namely, that of the association of *simple* impressions and ideas (if they are simple, how can they resemble each other?), and that of real connection, which is not a product but a condition of association (cf. pp. 168, 170). Here the real connection between love and the desire is dependent upon "the original constitution of the mind" and, "abstractly consider'd, is not necessary" (p. 368). Until he gets back to the genuine atomistic conclusion quoted in the text he flounders about, saying ingenuously that in these other considerations he "departs a little from that simplicity, which has hitherto been [the] principal force and beauty" of his system (p. 367).

Skinner makes a mistake comparable to Hume's (in the quotation in the text) when he translates, "I feel like playing cards," into "I feel as I often feel when I have started to play cards," (*About Behaviorism*, p. 28). The translation is at least approximately correct in that the two two sentences (may) have the same truth conditions. But have I learned by induction that the otherwise indescribable feeling I now have is like the one I have had in the past that has been relieved by playing cards, and therefore in all probability this feeling will be relieved in the same manner? That is possible only if it is conceivable that *this* feeling (which is now unnameable except as "the desire to play cards") might have got hooked up (by operant conditioning) to some other activity (and thereby become nameable as the desire to engage in *that* activity); for only under this condition is the connection between this feeling and the activity of playing cards a *causal* connection (either of cause to effect or, as Skinner [cf. *ibid.* p. 224] and presumably Hume believe, as mutually independent effects of a common cause).

Neither Hume nor Skinner takes seriously enough phenomenological and linguistic considerations of the way in which feelings and desires have concordant intentional objects so that it is logically *absurd* and not merely causally *false* to say "I satisfy my desire to play cards by playing the piano," and "I love my son so I hope he is in misery."

4: THE DIALECTIC OF ACTOR

AND SPECTATOR

We have by now seen the strengths and weaknesses of the explanations given by Spectator II, who holds all real explanation to be causal and who tolerates the reason explanations by Spectator I only in the interim before he fulfills his promise to explain all causally. His explanation does not spectacularly break down at some specific point of application to the child and to the other spectator or even in his accounts of his own past actions; but unless he exempts his present action of explaining, the whole business collapses. He must claim to be responding to evidence in obedience to rule, and not just responding to stimuli according to law.

"Self-exemption," though I have repeatedly used the word, is not perhaps the entirely appropriate name for the spectator's act of salvation. It is not that he finds that all events have causes, notices his paradox, and hastily adds "except my action of claiming this to be true." Hunting for causes is like hunting for game animals; the hunter does not have to extricate himself from the embarrassment he would be in had he foolishly counted himself a game animal. Rather, what makes wild animals game animals is that the hunter hunts them; it is his reasons and acts that create the classification "game animals." Not all animals are game animals, and no animals would be game animals unless someone hunted them. Just as there are rules for hunting that have been made by or for hunters, there are rules for determining what things are to count as causes. A hunter who disregards the laws defining game animals and follows Tom Lehrer's rule "If it moves, you shoot!" will end in suicide. A spectator who disregards his active role in obeying rules for finding causes and says simply that all actions are effects will end in self-stultification. But only when the physiologist wishes to *épater les bourgeois* or turns philosopher on a pompous occasion is he likely to put his conclusions into a form that is self-stultifying. Then he should be reminded of how he came to use the categories he employs in his explanations.

The primordial experience from which we project causal concepts onto occurrences in the world is that of making something happen, the resistance to effort, and the discovery that things happen without one's own operation upon them. Locke derives (very sketchily) the complex idea of cause from the reflective idea of power. Berkeley says that we have a direct awareness of causation in the acts of our own will and imagination, and in fact that is the only conception of causation with metaphysical truth, the ordinary scientific relation of causation being that of sign to subsequent idea. Even Hume, in passages that have usually been overlooked because of the greater importance attached to his criticisms of Berkeley, says, "It must, however, be confessed that the animal *nisus* which we experience . . . enters very much into that vulgar, inaccurate idea which is formed of [force and power]." [1] Maine de Biran derived the conception of causation from that of one's exertion and effort. The

1. *Enquiry Concerning Human Understanding*, ed. Hendel (New York, 1955), p. 79n. Consider also the important animadversions upon the different experiences of necessity had by the "agent" and by "any thinking being, who may consider the action" (namely, the spectator), *ibid.*, 103n. and *Treatise of Human Nature*, p. 408.

work of Piaget has destroyed the oversimplification of these armchair psychologists but agrees with their main point. He found that the child before the age of 8 already has seventeen categorially distinct paradigms of causation, some of which even point towards the classical Hume and Mach; but of the "phenomenistic" (roughly Humean) categorization, he "wonders whether [it] would exist if there were not other forms of relation to support it" found "in the mind of the very young child, *saturated as it is with dynamism, finalism, animism* . . . ," and so forth, which have to do directly with the child's activity before and during the time when the child gradually begins to recognize the polarity between himself and his world.[2]

If the dynamic component in our causal thought is derivative from our primordial sense of the difference between making something happen and the happening of something without our effort, the second component in causal conceptions—that of regularity—arises also from primordial experience of learning what else happens when we exert ourselves. I would not be able to make my unlearned bodily movements effective if I did not learn from experience that when I make the same bodily movements, the further consequences of what I do are much the same. Every time I make it happen that I strike a match, there is flame, and noticing this is what makes it possible for me to strike a match intentionally. I do one thing by doing another, or one thing in order that something else may ensue.

2. *The Child's Conception of Physical Causality* (New York, 1930), p. 260. Italics added. See also Cassirer, *The Philosophy of Symbolic Forms* (New Haven, 1955), 2:157, 200, 212.

Only a world that is regular in its sequence of happenings is a world in which intentions can be formed and executed. Only actions that have antici- pated consequences are actions that can be performed for reasons.

Whether acts themselves have causes is not yet the question; it suffices that they have effects. The agent is not concerned about whether causation *goes through* his action from past to future; it suffices that it extends from present act to future consequences. Knowledge of causation in the past, but not knowledge of the causes of present action, is embedded in plans for the future, and for the agent this knowledge determines his action only as a reason for doing one thing rather than another. Causal generalizations about the past can be rules for the future. Causal generalizations as rules are recipes for getting future things done intentionally. Only active, goal-directed agents can have the experi- ences that discover causal connections, and they alone can have any use for this knowledge.

With the growth of the agent's particular and peculiar individuality through participation in a social process of symbolically or actually occupying the point of view of another, or through his being a spectator of others' actions and their consequences, he is enabled to see the world as not just *his* surroundings with himself in the center. The primordial causal relations that were radial from his center of activity can now be seen obliquely, connecting things which have no active or practical connection with himself. Seen obliquely, the causal nexus connects things with each other, not things with oneself alone. The original egocentricity of causality is lost, and later even the anthropomorphic relics (such as forces) are deleted, leaving only regularity of sequence, concomitancy of variation, and counterfactual conditionality as the categorial structure of things and events in a causal system. In this process, "our notion of cause becomes correspondingly more elusive . . . [and] the language of cause tends to its own supersession." [3] The phenomenological origin of causal thinking in the actions of an agent is forgotten by the spectator who renounces animism, and the experience of agency from which it grew is itself finally declared illusory by the completely objective causal spectator. For him, agency as the ability to start new causal chains is dissolved into a meeting point of causal chains extending from the past into the future; there is no action, but only a sequence of mental and bodily states that instantiates causal regularities. What is left of the causal relation—concomitancy, counterfactual conditionality, and regularity—*goes through* the putative nucleus of agency, through the agent who appears to himself to spontaneously initiate new causal sequences. "There is no place in the scientific position for a self as a true originator or initiator of action." [4]

But since being a spectator and explainer is a role that an agent assumes, it is not to be wondered at that he does not dissolve *himself* in the powerful solvent of causal analysis. Causation extending from antecedent conditions through decision to execution is a concept applied only to actors and applied only by spectators

3. Max Black, "Making Things Happen," in *Determinism and Freedom*, ed. Sidney Hook (New York, 1958), p. 29.

4. B. F. Skinner, *About Behaviorism*, p. 225.

who are agents who make it happen that causal explanations are given because they have good reason to do so. It is only by what Kierkegaard attributed to Hegel—"a fit of transcendental absent-mindedness"— that an active creative spectator can say there is no action but only reaction.

The agent who is Spectator II says

(1) E is evidence that C, prior to action by actor, causes actor to decide to do A.

His saying this, like the actor's decision to do A, must have a cause, so he asserts

(2) C' is the cause of my saying (1)

and he must have evidence for this if his statement is to be creditable, namely,

(3) E' is my evidence for (2).

The agent-spectator is in an infinite regress unless he exempts himself by claiming to dwell in a context of explanation which cannot (like everyone else's) be discounted in an explained context. His evidence, which gives creditability to his explanation, is always one step ahead of the causality for which he has evidence.[5]

5. Skinner is aware of the bizarreness of self-exemption and denies (*About Behaviorism*, p. 234) that he has to resort to it. But I am not sure he succeeds. He says that the designer of a culture (that is, Skinner) will always be culture-bound "since he will not be able to free himself *entirely* from the predispositions which have been engendered by the environment in which he has lived" (*Beyond Freedom and Dignity*, p. 164). I have italicized *entirely;* to be non-self-exemptive "entirely" should have been omitted, and then we would have had only Skinner's behavior on the

But the spectator does not *know* a priori that he will discover causes for the actions of the actor he observes. He takes it as a postulate and would close up shop if he did not believe it; but he does not know it. The regularities he and we find in the world may be on only one stratum; any causal filter lets many events go unexplained, though we believe we can make the meshes finer and finer. Our primitive causal conceptions were formulated to control only the middle-sized objects of common sense for which we have practical use, and common sense is not frustrated by the fact that most things we see are things for which common sense has not the most distant knowledge of causes. Our refined causal conceptions are designed to master isolated systems of operationally defined variables; but since in reality there are no isolated systems in which all parameters are controlled, our causal laws, which are supposed to be unexceptional, have, in fact,

same epistemological level as that of other culture-builders he condemns, and his pigeons. Again (*About Behaviorism*, p. 235), he says, "A proposition is 'true' to the extent that with its help the listener responds effectively to the situation it describes." The scare-quotes around *true* are a sign of self-exemption; what he says is true (no quotes), but what passes for "true" in the explained context is that which is effective in the actor's adaptive and preparatory behavior. That it is adaptive for Skinner does not mean that it is unquotedly true. In *Verbal Behavior* (New York, 1957), p. 456, facing a challenge from Russell in *Inquiry into Meaning and Truth* (New York, 1940), p. 14, that is very much like this one, Skinner claims that his verbal behavior is like that of his subjects and is to be judged by the same standards, saying that "In many ways, then, this seems to me to be a better way of talking about verbal behavior, and that is why I have tried to get the reader to talk about it in this way too. But have I told him the truth? Who can say? A science of verbal behavior probably makes no provision for truth or certainty (but we cannot even be certain of the truth of that)." So we are left with "truth" but not with truth.

empirically only statistical validity, with complete causal determinism at best only an asymptotic ideal and, indeed, an ideal now not even worth pursuing in the most advanced sciences. The doctrine that all events in the world are causally necessitated by antecedent or concurrent events or states is both unfalsifiable and unconfirmable. However it may be from the angel's point of view, we human beings who are spectators follow a program of looking for causes without any guarantee that we will succeed. I know I will not (logically cannot) succeed in one specific instance, namely the event of my saying that I have done so. If the difficulties outlined in my previous discussion (we kill in order to dissect) could be overcome, *I* might succeed in finding the causally sufficient conditions for *your* saying you have found a causal explanation of *my* utterances, and *you* might succeed in finding the causally sufficient conditions for *my* saying this; the angel might know that both of us are right, if we are; but you and I cannot know it.

An argument like that of Ewing against solipsism might be renewed here to show that if I exempt myself from my own causal explanations in order not to stultify my argument, I have as good reason to exempt you from causal explanation in order not to have to discount your argument. But that short way will not work here, for I cannot candidly say that I do not often think other people's decisions and actions are causally explicable. I often agree with Spinoza that "experience teaches us no less clearly than reason, that men believe themselves free simply because they are conscious of their actions and unconscious of the causes whereby those actions are determined." [6] And with Mephistopheles: "Du glaubst zu schieben und du wirst geschoben." [7] But it is an open question whether Spinoza and Mephistopheles were right; I certainly have not succeeded in finding specific causal explanations of the *soi-disant* decisions and actions of other people. I have not succeeded because I have not tried hard enough; or because behavioral effects and actions are complementary, like waves and particles in light, so that the conditions for the discovery of the one exclude the possibility of discovery of the other; or because they are not there to be found. Until or unless I succeed in finding them, the possibility is always open that they are not there to be found, however intellectually frustrating this prospect must be.

It may be objected that such tychistic faintheartedness is too high a price to pay for an understanding of action, especially since it has been argued (by Hume and Schlick)[8] that it is more difficult to justify the ascription of free agency to someone when it is assumed that his action has no cause than when the contrary assumption is made. If the reign of causal law seems to exclude freedom, the denial of it seems to imply chaos and the impossibility of imputing actions to agents.

This is a false dilemma, but not merely for the

6. *Ethics*, book 3, proposition 2, note.

7. "You think you push, but you are pushed."

8. *Treatise of Human Nature*, pp. 404, 411–12; *Problems of Ethics* (New York, 1939), pp. 156–58.

reasons given by Hume and Mill,[9] namely that "caused behavior" does not mean "coerced or necessitated behavior"; the dilemma is false because it supposes that "liberty of action" means "uncaused behavior," which in turn means "inexplicable and therefore nonimputable behavior." This is false; an action done for a reason has as secure a place in an intelligible order as an event that is caused and need not be any more surprising or unpredictable. We are rightly told that acts "due to chance" cannot be imputed to the agent, as if "due to chance" meant simply "without cause." But, as Aristotle pointed out,[10] "due to chance" does not mean "without cause," but "without reason." Of one kind of action it makes sense to say that it was done by chance, namely, of an action undertaken under one description (I intentionally put on my coat) but having also post facto another description (I by chance broke the vase). The latter assertion cannot inculpate me (except perhaps for carelessness), for I cannot undertake to do a careless action.

The issue raised in Hume's argument, however, is not the explanation of this kind of inadvertent action, but turns on the distinction between a *caused decision* and a *decision made by chance*. But here again the dilemma is invalid because "chance decision" (if it means anything) does not mean "uncaused decision." Obviously I cannot *decide to break the vase by chance*. Can I *decide by chance* to break the vase? It sounds odd to say this, but it could be truly said under one of the

9. *Treatise of Human Nature*, 404–6; *System of Logic* (New York, 1848), p. 523.

10. *Physics*, book 2, chapter 5.

following conditions: I decide to break something and, by chance, the vase is the handiest thing; or I decide to let a chance event, a flip of a coin, tell me whether to break it or not. If we wish to describe these as fortuitous decisions to break the vase, nothing is said about whether they have causes or not. In fact, it may well be that such "chance decisions" are more transparently caused than decisions we ascribe to reasons.

But the relation between explanation by causes and explanation by reasons is too deep to be exposed by attention merely to this idiom. We must, rather, examine the rival methodologies of the two kinds of explanation.

The things actors do for which I have had some success in determining causes are bits of behavior that are not actions and actions for which they had no good reason, or in ordinary parlance, "no reason." I can ask for and frequently find, at least schematically, the causes of someone's making a mistake in arithmetic; but I do not ask for, nor do I generally know, the causes of his getting the right answer. To understand all causally is to forgive all; Sartre says, "Psychological determinism . . . is . . . an attitude of excuse." [11] When an actor does a thing for a reason I believe he has, lack of knowledge of cause or even a claim to know that there was not a cause but only a reason does not lead me to say his action was fortuitous. It does not even make it less predictable than it would have been had it had a cause which I did know. Most of the practically important predictions I make about other

11. *Being and Nothingness* (New York, 1956), p. 40.

people are based upon my knowledge of their reasons, and very little upon my knowledge of the causes that are effective in their behavior. *There is an inverse relation between the ascription of reasons and the specification of causes;* only the fact that our knowledge of both is schematic and often vague permits us to feel comfortable in giving one kind of explanation without revoking the other. But if one *knows* the causes of a man's behavior, for example, the rug slipped and caused him to fall, only a very suspicious psychiatrist will still want to know his reasons for his falling. Only a diplomat as distrustful as Metternich would say, when he heard that Talleyrand had died, "I wonder what he meant by doing *that!*"

The test of understanding something is whether the ground is prepared for more knowledge, whether it protects us against surprise. *Savoir pour prévoir.* Prediction or retrodiction is the public test. Human behavior can be predicted or retrodicted on two grounds: understanding causes, or understanding reasons. We employ sometimes one and sometimes the other; schematically we may believe both, but we never in fact cash in on both these schemata at the same time, for to get the specific knowledge needed for a causal prediction requires such restraints on the actor that the effectiveness of any reasons he might have is abrogated, while to allow him to act, to go his own way, defeats our efforts to discover specific causes. There is thus a dialectic between Spectator I and Spectator II, and every victory of one is a defeat for the other.

But what of the child, the agent in our little episode? How does he stand vis-à-vis the quarreling spectators, like Hans Castorp between Naphta and Settembrini fighting for his soul?

It is obvious that the agent must reject the claims of the second spectator. He will not convince Spectator II that he is right in doing so, for his rejection is an item of his behavior that Spectator II thinks he can handle just as he handled everything else the child did. The child may, thereby, be dispirited just as William James was when he feared that he was nothing but an "interesting mechanism." Every advance that Spectator II makes in his knowledge of the causes of the child's behavior seems to destroy one more illusion the child has that it is up to him to do one thing or another; someone, namely Spectator II, already knows which he will do, and this makes the child believe that his options are more limited than he previously thought, or are even closed. Every advance of causal knowledge seems to constrict the scope of free action.

We can understand, perhaps we have experienced, the threat to dignity and freedom that seems implicit in the advances made in causal knowledge of ourselves. If someone knows (or even *could* know) the agent's present state and a causal law that links it necessarily to his past and future states, even though in making the transition from present to future state the agent must suffer through a period of deliberation, then deliberation, though inescapable, makes no difference to the outcome. It had to occur as it did, and it had to produce the outcome it did. Whoever knows this may feel, as James did, that the conviction of spontaneity, freedom, option, and responsibility that pervades the deliberation and remorse that sometimes follows it are delusive. If the agent had causal knowledge of the outcome, he could not deliberate, for as Aristotle pointed out, one can deliberate only about what may be brought to happen, not about what will occur no matter what. One who had this knowledge would not even have the illusion of deciding; at most he would predict. No one has this knowledge about himself, but the agent may well suppose that someone else (the angel, or Spectator II) has it. What effect does this have on his experience of deliberating, deciding, and acting? It does not lessen the urgency of his deliberation or the difficulty of his decision since he does not know *what* the prediction is. He has to work out the problem that the spectator worked out, but he works it out under the illusory rubric of reaching a decision, while the spectator worked it out under the rubric of a causal explanation leading to a prediction. Many Calvinist writers have put an oblique interpretation upon their experience of decision, seeing it more as a process of discovering a plan than as a process of making a plan. For one who is not comforted by seeing himself as acting a role in a divine drama, there remains the ironic spectacle that his agonizing decisions and someone else's disinterested predictions always turn out to be the same.

The angel looking down on the scene may be moved by pity for the agent, a self-deluded interesting mechanism, an impotent and miserable puppet. But if the angel agrees with the argument I am about to give, he will tell the agent: Do not be disheartened; you are deluded if you believe that the spectator knows a causal law you conform to willy-nilly; the spectator does not know and cannot know such a law.

Let me explain this solacing message. The spectator by induction[12] has been able to establish the truth of law L: "Actors in state S under condition C do A." The evidence for this is observation of actors in state S and under condition C. But the agent who feels impotent is not in state S, because he correctly believes that the spectator knows law L, while none of the actors in the population from which this induction was made could have believed it, for the spectator did not know there was this law until the induction had been made. The present agent is, by that very fact, not in state S, and hence law L does not foretell that he will do A. The agent perks up when he hears this, but soon his suspicion returns. "Surely," he will say, "the spectator has taken care of this, since I am not the only one who has felt this way—Omar Khayyám, William James, and John Stuart Mill,[13] among others, did. There must be *another* law." And indeed the spectator has made an induction from this subset and derived law L': "Agents in state S' (S modified by knowledge of L) under condition C do A'." But however many sublaws there are, applying in succession to agents who

12. I do not wish this sequence of arguments to leave the impression that I think laws of nature, including psychological laws, can be established only by perfect induction. To be sure, the problem discussed here arises most saliently under an all-or-none conception of laws instead of under a statistical or hypothetico-deductive conception. The difficulties that I try to uncover in causal laws of action are independent of the specific methodology by which they are established.

13. This was a phase in Mill's crisis too; see *Autobiography* (Oxford, 1924), p. 143.

know L', L'', and so on, as long as the last law is known only to the spectator, the agent does not have any reason to believe that the spectator is in possession of a law that applies to *him*, and he regains an at least delusory feeling of the significance of deliberation and decision. He may not be free from the necessity of acting in a predicted way (for there may be a law L''' that applies to him); but not knowing its existence and correctness, at least he need not feel neurotically paralyzed.

But suppose our agent does have good access to knowledge of what the spectator is doing, and finds that L''' has been applicable to him up to now, and L''' is the latest generalization the spectator has drawn. Now he is really free from *any* causal law actually known to hold, for there is not yet known to be a causal law which applies to him and which gives someone else an inference ticket to his decisions and actions. This story can be repeated an indefinite number of times but always with the same outcome: the agent, if he knows as much as the spectator, can always stay one jump ahead of the spectator's claim, for his knowledge puts him into a different state from that of those who inductively supported the claim made by the spectator. If anyone knows such a law that has the feared consequences, it must be someone with knowledge of a sequence of laws each more specific than the one before it and with the last law known without induction. Only such a series of laws and a law known noninductively could catch the agent in a causal net; and no human being knows whether there is such a law or not, that is, whether causal determinism is metaphysically true or not.

Our human sympathy with the child is thus misplaced, for the child either does not know he is in an antinomy of cause and freedom, or he can escape from it. The agent who does not know that the spectator can predict his action lives in no anxiety that all his decisions have already been predicted; and the agent who does know that the spectator makes this claim is immune to it, because he is not like the actors whose behavior provided the evidence for the spectator's claim. The agent who knows this can always do some action which will surprise the spectator. He is in a position like that of the spectator; both agent and spectator have it in their power to exempt themselves from a causal discount of their decisions.

Every scientific spectator of human affairs knows this problem under the name of the Oedipus effect or self-defeating prophecy. But the ramifications of the problem are deeper than the ordinary methodological precautions that a wise experimenter takes against it. We have already explained how laws of nature may become rules of action; here we have an extreme case of it, raised to its highest potential. Kant says of a rational being that it is one that can act according to a *conception* of a law. This may be accomplished by obedience to the law, by breaking the law, or by acting so as to exempt oneself from the application of the law. Any series of supervenient laws that are meant to deal in a causal way with the self-defeating prediction can be dealt with by the agent in the same way he dealt with the first law: he can exempt himself from it by staying always one step ahead of the spectator held back by his inductions from actors less knowledgeable than he. He exempts himself in the same manner that the spectator as agent exempts himself from the last law of which he is the author.

Only the social sciences face the problem of self-defeating predictions. Only human beings have the capacity to change with understanding, to step back and thereby enlarge the area of action open to them. So long as the actor is confined to the explained context, the more the spectator knows the more rigidly the actor conforms to the spectator's expectations. It is the ghost of the all-knowing spectator that seems to threaten the spontaneity, freedom, and dignity of the agent; every increase in the spectator's causal knowledge reduces alternative contingencies and closes off some option the actor thinks he has. But the same facts that close options for the actor when known only to the spectator can open new lines of action when known by the agent. The only knowledge which threatens him is that which someone else possesses and he lacks. Men unwittingly conform to causal laws and confirm causal predictions until they gain knowledge that this is what they are doing; only then can they take steps against doing so, or freely do what they otherwise would do unfreely. Self-knowledge is a condition for eluding spectator-knowledge; it is a condition for freedom.

The man who is free is one who stepped out of his role as an actor whose lines are dictated by someone else's interests, knowledge, and control. But each man is also a spectator of himself, certainly of his past and of the broad outlines of his probable future; even as actor for himself as spectator, doing what he expects of himself, he may not be free, may not act "in good faith" but only maintain a false front to himself. Hence this stepping out of a role may not be merely an escape from the rigid prognoses of psychological determinists; it may be an ethical act of self-criticism, of judging and even reforming (re-forming) oneself. It might even be appropriately described in religious terms as a revolution in the heart, a rebirth by which the new man emerges from the old and acts as if his past were no burden he has to bear. "This backward-stepping can never be closed to us," writes Stuart Hampshire.[14] A man *can* always be free. But he has to *make himself free* by taking this step backward, looking upon his former self as an actor playing a role the agent now rejects or freely accepts. Compared with this inexplicable act of emancipation, the exemption from self-stultification in epistemology is an affair of the study, of concern only to the philosopher.

I called this act of self-emancipation from any assigned role inexplicable. I did so hesitantly and reluctantly; my bent is not to traffic in mysteries, so I must try, like Kant, to explain not the act but the act's inexplicability.[15] I have already argued that the act cannot be explained causally, but neither can it be explained by giving reasons for it, for this would entail an infinite regress of reasons, and the act would never be done if it were done and justified only with an

14. *Thought and Action* (London, 1960), p. 190.
15. *Foundations of the Metaphysics of Morals*, last sentence.

antecedent sufficient reason. Yet having reasons is not therefore unreasonable. The act I am now talking about is that of committing oneself to reason, and that is defensible before the bar of reason, which is erected just by such acts performed in the society of human beings. The process is not an infinite regress, but a circle. This particular kind of circle is known as dialectic.

Let us first examine this obscure process on a very primitive level, one so primitive that none of us can remember being on it, but a level that each of us must have passed through in becoming a person. Origins are obscure and we can only conjecture about them. But Hegel, in tracing the steps by which our species became rational political animals, and George Herbert Mead, in tracing the steps by which the infant becomes a personal agent, have told comparable stories. But where Hegel sees the turning point in mortal combat, Mead sees it in playing a game.

Hegel writes of the beginning of hierarchical order in a Hobbesian state of nature; but what emerges is not Hobbesian man tamed, but men in their diverse stations, each with its duties and characteristic form of self-consciousness. After recounting the deadly conflict in which one man dominates another but allows him to live in order to have work done and to enjoy his own mastery, Hegel writes: "Precisely in labor where there seemed to be merely some outsider's mind and ideas involved, the bondsman becomes aware, through this re-discovery of himself by himself, of having and being 'a mind of his own.' " [16] Mead would agree with all

16. *Phenomenology of Mind* (London and New York, 1949), p. 239.

this except calling it a "re-discovery"; it is not even a discovery, but an invention that must be reduced to practice. In play and the conversation of gestures and sounds, my actions are stimuli whose meaning is the response that another makes to them, but they are self-stimulating, too (since I also see and hear them), and I respond to my own acts in the way I see others respond to them; thus I come to see myself and my actions as others see them. "The attitudes of others which [I] assume as affecting [my] own conduct constitute the 'me', and that is something that is there, *but [my] response to it is as yet not given*." I respond to my self ('me') as another responds to it, "by taking part in [my] own conversation [of sound and gesture] with others, being aware of what [I am] saying and using that awareness of what [I am] saying *to determine what [I am] going to say thereafter*." [17] A person who can see himself as actor is not a mere biological organism any more; he is an agent responding not in an animal way to stimuli in automatic and predetermined ways ("the response is not yet given") but by participating in a symbolic process guided by assessing meanings of what has been done and observed ("determining what one is going to say thereafter").

Much as Hegel, Mead, and Cassirer have contributed to our understanding of this great transition from reaction to action, from automatism to symbolism, it still does not seem to me to be clearly enough understood to illuminate the better known process of mature dialectic, and I mention it only to show that

17. *Mind, Self & Society* (Chicago, 1934), pp. 176, 140. Italics added.

there may be deeper roots, in the way the *animal symbolicum* came to be, for that familiar process of social dialectic by which ethical and intellectual growth is accomplished. The "stepping back" from a response not yet given, the awareness of what one is doing to determine what one is going to do thereafter is characteristic of all our search for reasons. So let us turn to more familiar examples.

I claim I have a reason for something that I do; I do not claim necessarily that I have a reason for having this reason. Though I may do so, for example, in giving a geometrical proof, I sooner or later come to a reason that has no prior reason. But even of that I can ask: is it a good reason, or has my whole regression led to the discovery that I was rational about the little things but foolish about the whole? Generally men ask this question of themselves less than they are asked by others, for one man's good reason, never doubted but not indubitable, may for another be a poor reason, a pseudo-reason, a "rationalization."

Thereby ensues a dialogue, in which Spectator I becomes a teacher, critic, collaborator in a context that is no longer an asymmetrical inclusion of an explained context in an explanatory context, but one of equality in which what is a good reason for one ought to be acknowledged to be a good reason by the other. In this equality, there is no mounting a vertical infinite regress, but a pursuit of horizontal agreement in which one man's reasons may become those of another by a free interchange. Each man steps back and distances himself from his former acts, which he sees and interprets as if they were acts of another.

Consider a simple interaction between the child and Spectator I. Spectator I (now no longer a mere spectator, but a co-actor) asks the child: "What is the next number in the sequence 2, 4, 6, x?" He expects the child to answer "8," but not because he knows the state of the child's brain when the question is asked and causally predicts that that state will be followed by the state which causes the child to utter "8"; Spectator I is not playing the game Spectator II played, but gives his prediction on noncausal grounds, making a normative prediction because he knows the rules of arithmetic that are normative for the child's action. But the child astonishes him by answering "12," and, asked the reason, the child says "12 is to 6 as 4 is to 2." That is *a* right answer, but reached by a different norm from the one that guided the spectator's prediction. It is a norm that the spectator did not think of, and he now sees an ambiguity in his question that he had not noticed before. The spectator learns that his own good reason was not a good enough reason, and he can show the child that the child's good reason was not good enough, by showing him the difference between a progression and a proportion. Each learns something about himself, about the other, and about arithmetic.

Something like this goes on in all our social intercourse once the artificial constraints and asymmetries of the experimental situation are relaxed, and all the good reasons are not kept the secret possession of the spectator. My reasons lead to my actions; my actions become your reasons for your response; your response is a reason for my next action, which does not follow merely from the reason I originally had, but from my reason as modified by yours; gradually my original reason may be revoked, just as yours may be, under the guidance of the principle that a good reason is a reason that holds its own in social intercourse and cooperation. Good reasons become anonymous or vicariously valid, and the better they are the more anonymously weighty they are.

This process of dialectic is very different from that of persuasion. Persuasion is asymmetrical and may be causally mediated; in it, motives and intentions may not be shared but manipulated. Dialectic is mutual criticism of free and equal beings willing both to support and to change their reasons, actions, projects, plans, desires, and aspirations. In dialogue, I respect you as a free agent by using no argument and appealing to no reason to which I do not bind myself. I expose myself to your correction. If I do not regard you as a free agent and my equal, persuasion through manipulation of causes of your behavior may increase my power to elicit your agreement with me, but while increasing my power it adds nothing to the credentials of my reasons. Unlike Spectator II whose causal prediction could be confirmed only if he withheld his reasons for it from the agent, I want you to know both my reasons and better reasons than I know, for only then can your response be rightly normative for me. If my reasons are kept from you, your agreement is worthless to me; if I am kept in the dark about your reasons, then I cannot, or at least ought not, accept your actions as normative for me. The whole apparatus of control, necessary and allowable in experiment and persuasion, is out of place here; for my emancipation from the limitations of my role I need the criticism or backing of free men; only from them can I learn. The dialectic can go on forever but does not involve an infinite regress, for at each stage of agreement our shared reasons have passed the only tests to which they can have been subjected. We call the ultimate free acts of men rational when they keep the way open for us to reason together further.

I am not sure that my words "ultimate free acts" are quite apt. They suggest a unique action of turning over a new leaf, of freeing ourselves from all our yesterdays. So inexplicable is the act, when considered as the *salto mortale* of religious conversion by which that which was sown in corruption is raised in incorruption, that it has been seen not as an act of man at all, but as a gratuitous act of God. As an act, it is so mysterious as to be describable only tautologically, as deciding to decide, finding a reason to be reasonable, freely deciding to be free.

But perhaps it is just the talk of it as if it were a single act, done once and for all, which has misled me into this uncomfortable talk of mystery when I am discussing what is in fact the most familiar thing in a good life. I should be talking of a *style* of acting. To be reasonable is not something one decides to do tomorrow; it is a *way* of acting to be maintained, not an episode in a role to be assumed. It is a state of personal being expressed in how a man thinks, what ideals he pursues, and how he treats others. It is not a single step that takes him from being an interesting mechanism to being a person, but an enlargement of the person by repeatedly stepping back from what is given, finished, and done, in order better to pursue knowledge, beauty, and justice and to enjoy affection. Each stepping back divides life into two parts: prologue and adventure. *Reculez pour mieux sauter:*

> Civilization is 'dialectical' as well as dramatic. It is no simple event, no peaceful unwinding. Instead, it is an act, which it is forever necessary to begin anew; and its goal is never certain.[18]

18. Cassirer, *The Logic of the Humanities* (New Haven, 1961), p. 190.

BIBLIOGRAPHICAL NOTE

I have refrained from citing most writings in the vast current literature of the philosophy of action, though my debts to other writers, both those I agree with and those I disagree with, will be obvious; to have done so occasionally would have been invidious, and to have done so regularly would have covered half of each page with footnotes. A good bibliography by Robert McGowan and Myron Gochnauer will be found in *Agent, Action and Reason* edited by Robert Binkley, Richard Bronough, and Ausinio Marras (Toronto, 1971).

The dramaturgical model for the understanding of action has been used thematically by Kenneth Burke in *A Grammar of Motives* (Englewood Cliffs, N.J., 1941), Erving Goffman in *The Presentation of the Self in Everyday Life* (Garden City, N.Y., 1959), Rom Harré and P. F. Secord in *The Explanation of Social Behavior* (Totowa, N.J., 1973), Victor Turner in *Dramas, Fields, and Metaphors* (Ithaca, N.Y., 1974), and (with a somewhat different focus) Maurice Natanson in "Man as an Actor," *Philosophy and Phenomenological Research* 26 (1966): 327–41. *The Monist*, vol. 69, no. 2 (1965), contained ten articles on the theme "Agent and Spectator."

Peter Jones's *Philosophy and the Novel* (Oxford, 1975), with its sustained analogy between understanding a person, understanding a novel, and understanding an argument, was published too late for me to make use of it in this work. For the same reason I was not able to profit from Stephen Toulmin's critique of the dramaturgical model in *Understanding Human Persons*, ed. Theodore Mischel (Oxford, 1974), pp. 185–216, especially pp. 207–14.

INDEX OF NAMES

141